# TOTALLY
# USELESS
# INFORMATION

Publications International, Ltd.

**CONTRIBUTING WRITERS:** Jeff Bahr, Ryan Cole, Helen Davies, Colleen Delegan, Tom DiMichael, Katherine Don, James Duplacey, Emily Dwass, David Gerardi, Jonathan W. Jordan, Jonathan Kelly, Rhonda Markowitz, Art Montague, Kimberly Morris, Ed Moser, Robert Norris, Eric Peterson, David Priess, J.R. Raphael, Lawrence Robinson, Bill Sasser, Lexi M. Schuh, Paul Seaburn, Ken Sheldon, Allen Smith, Bryant Smith, Dan Spellerberg, Ilene Springer, Jennifer Wilkinson, Chuck Wills, Kelly Wingard

**COVER ART:** Shutterstock.com

**INTERIOR ART:** **Art Explosion:** 24, 25, 30, 46, 57, 58, 61, 70, 72, 74, 75, 76, 79, 81, 83, 89, 96, 99, 109, 115, 117, 119, 121, 124, 125, 129, 130, 133, 134, 135, 139, 150, 152, 153, 155, 156, 172, 174, 177, 180, 180, 181, 184, 184, 187, 189, 191, 201, 202, 205, 205, 206, 207, 208, 209, 211, 217, 221, 225, 226, 227, 228, 229, 232, 233, 245, 248, 249, 253, 260, 261; **Clipart.com:** 120, 178, 244, 259, 269; **Dreamstime:** 105, 143; **Getty:** 94, 106, 108, 110, 114, 136, 165, 166, 167, 263, 272; **Shutterstock.com:** 5, 6, 8, 9, 11, 16, 20, 29, 39, 41, 42, 52, 61, 63, 73, 77, 84, 85, 91, 123, 127, 132, 138, 141, 158, 160, 161, 163, 164, 166, 168, 169, 170, 173, 175, 179, 182, 183, 186, 187, 193, 196, 197, 200, 210, 212, 214, 215, 218, 219, 234, 235, 239, 242, 243, 247, 250, 256, 257

Louis Weber, CEO
Publications International, Ltd.
8140 Lehigh Avenue
Morton Grove, IL 60053

# TABLE OF CONTENTS

# Why Do Cats Purr?

Felines are forever mysterious to mere humans. One of our favorite ponderings is the act of purring.

Don't cats purr because they're content? When cats purr, people are happy. But cats aren't always happy when they purr. There are actually several reasons why cats purr, and happiness is only one of them. Purring begins at birth and is a vital form of communication between mother and kitten. The kitten purrs to let its mother know it's getting enough milk, and the mother cat purrs back to reassure her kitten.

What's the significance of purring? Cats purr throughout their lives and often at times you wouldn't expect. Cats purr when they are frightened, ill, or injured, and they even purr while giving birth. Animal behaviorists believe that cats purr under stressful conditions to comfort themselves and to signal their feelings to other cats. A frightened cat may purr to indicate that it is being submissive or non-threatening, and an aggressive cat may purr to let other cats know that it will not attack. Some cats purr even when they're dying.

Interestingly, domestic cats aren't the only felines that purr. Some of the big cats—lions, cougars, and cheetahs—also exhibit this endearing behavior. But it's much more soothing—not to mention safer—to stroke a purring pet cat than the king of the jungle.

## ANIMALS BY THE BUNCH

Here are the official collective names for various groups of critters:

- a bale of turtles
- a bevy of quails
- a blessing of unicorns
- a business of ferrets
- a cackle of hyenas
- a charm of finches
- a clowder of cats
- a congregation of alligators
- a covey of partridges
- a crash of rhinoceroses
- an exaltation of larks
- a fall of woodcocks
- a flamboyance of flamingoes
- a gaze of raccoons
- a hover of trout
- a husk of jackrabbits
- a leap of leopards
- a murder of magpies
- an ostentation of peacocks
- a parliament of owls
- a passel of possum
- a prickle of porcupines
- a rhumba of rattlesnakes
- a romp of otters
- a shrewdness of apes
- a smack of jellyfish
- a streak of tigers
- a string of ponies
- a swarm of eels
- a troop of kangaroos
- a troubling of goldfish
- a wisdom of wombats
- a zeal of zebras

# Do Snakes Slither Up Into Toilets?

We hesitate to tell you this, since it might lead to a lifetime of bathroom paranoia, but snakes (and other nasty animals) do climb up through toilets now and again. And yes, some have bitten people who have been going about their "business."

There are two ways for an animal to make its way up into your toilet. First, if your house is connected to a municipal sewer system, the drain leading from your toilet connects to a large network of pipes that go all the way to a sewer treatment plant. This network has many small entry points, including manholes and other people's toilets.

Because of the food everyone washes down the sink, these pipes are popular hangouts for rats; because there are delicious rats everywhere, the pipes are also popular with snakes. Water rarely fills the pipes all the way and usually moves slowly, so snakes and rats can come and go as they please. Every once in a while, a snake or a rat will follow a pipe all the way to a toilet, swim through the little bit of water in the bowl, and pop out to see what's going on.

The second way in is much quicker. Most houses have vents that run from the sewage drainpipes to the roof. These allow noxious sewer gas to escape without stinking up the house. If these vents aren't covered, rats, snakes, frogs, and even squirrels can fall in and land unexpectedly in the main drain line. They scurry for the nearest exit: the toilet. (It's probably a good idea to cover those vents if you haven't already.)

There have been many reported cases of unexpected toilet visitors, including a venomous water moccasin that bit a Jacksonville, Florida, woman in 2005 and a baby brush-tailed possum that crawled out of a toilet in Brisbane, Australia, in 2008. If you have a snake phobia, the creepiest story might be that of Keith, a ten-foot-long boa constrictor that kept poking out of toilets in an apartment building in Manchester, England, in 2005. The snake, a pet that its owner had set free after being evicted, lived the high life, eating sewer rats and freaking people out for months before a building resident lured him into a bucket.

Take this as a warning not to dilly-dally for too long in the bathroom. There are safer places to catch up on your reading.

# DEADLIEST CREEPY CRAWLIES

Insect stings kill between 40 and 100 Americans every year. But in other parts of the world, bugs kill many times that number. Here are some of the most fearsome.

**LOCUSTS:** Individually, locusts are just weird-looking grasshoppers. But when they swarm, look out! Locusts can rapidly devastate huge regions of farmland, leading to mass starvation.

**MOSQUITOES:** Believe it or not, mosquitoes are responsible for more deaths than any other creature. The reason? They spread a wide variety of potentially deadly diseases including malaria, which kills an estimated two million people annually.

**AFRICANIZED BEES:** Big honeybees with a really bad attitude, Africanized bees attack with little provocation. Worse, when one bee stings, it releases a chemical that provokes the entire nest.

**FLEAS:** Little more than a nuisance today, fleas are one of history's greatest mass killers. Fleas are thought to have wiped out one-third of the population of Europe through the transmission of bubonic plague in the 14th century.

**BRAZILIAN WANDERING SPIDER:** The most venomous spider in the world, this deadly nocturnal hunter likes to hide in banana bunches during the day. One bite, and you're in big trouble.

**BLACK WIDOW:** Another deadly arachnid, the venom of the black widow is more powerful than that of the cobra or the coral snake.

**SYDNEY FUNNEL-WEB SPIDER:** Indigenous to Australia, this venomous spider has fangs strong enough to puncture shoes.

**TSETSE FLY:** This harmless-looking bug is responsible for spreading sleeping sickness throughout Africa, resulting in hundreds of deaths each year.

## When Do Fish Sleep?

It's hard to tell whether fish are sleeping because they don't have eyelids. That's why you'll never win a staring contest with your pet goldfish—its eyes are always open.

So how do fish get their beauty sleep? They don't, at least not in the way we humans do. Their body functions slow down and they get a bit dozy, but they're generally still alert enough to scatter when danger arises. You could say that they're having a relaxing daydream, but they never actually fall into a deep sleep.

Some fish simply float motionless in the water as they doze; others, such as grouper and rockfish, rest against rocks or plants. The craftier varieties, like bass and perch, hole up underneath rocks and logs or hide in crevices. Others stay on the move while in a daze, recharging without ever stopping.

In the 1930s, biologist David Graham watched a fish sleeping upright on its tail for an hour or so. Then Graham turned on the lights, and the fish jerked back into a swimming position and darted around. It was the aquatic equivalent of being caught napping in school.

When exactly do fish rest? It varies from species to species. Most fish rely on the weak light from the surface to see, and since that light pretty much disappears at night, it's thought that a lot of fish do their resting then. However, some fish rest during the day, while others do so randomly. There are, it seems, no set bedtimes in the fish world.

# SWEATING LIKE A DOG

It's hot out, and you and your dog are taking a midday run. As your shirt becomes soaked with perspiration, Rover breaks a sweat in his own way—by panting. That's what you've always thought, anyway.

Dogs don't sweat by panting, but they do regulate their body temperature that way. They release excess heat through their tongues while taking short, rapid breaths—sometimes as many as 300 to 400 per minute. This process expels hot air from their lungs and body cavities. But because such breathing is quick and shallow, it doesn't use up much energy, so the dog doesn't risk overheating more.

It's widely thought that dogs don't sweat at all, but that's not true either. Although humans perspire through our skin, a dog's fur prevents the release of moisture and heat. Our canine companions lack the extensive sweat glands that we have, but they do have some—and they're located in their foot pads. That's why you can see pad prints on wood floors and outdoor decks in warm weather. That's also why your pet's paws can smell kind of funky, like armpits. As humans do, dogs perspire when they get overheated or anxious. We get sweaty pits, they get sweaty paws.

However, the paws of a dog are too small to release the excessive body heat generated during a vigorous romp in the middle of summer. That's when the tongue flops out. With both cooling systems in operation, a dog is so efficient at lowering its body temperature that it can endure prolonged, high-speed chases—in pursuit of a rabbit, say—without the need to stop. The rabbit, on the other hand, has no such means to cool down. Sure, it'll keep running to evade the dog, but it'll likely drop dead from heat exhaustion in the process.

# ALL CREATURES GREAT AND OBSCURE

The animal kingdom is vast and varied, full of exotic specimens such as giraffes, penguins, and monkeys. Yet, there are quite a few other inhabitants of the animal kingdom that you've probably never heard of. Here are a few that might fascinate and amaze you.

**RACCOON DOG:** Named for the similarity in appearance to that of a raccoon, this solitary creature is actually an omnivorous member of the canine family. Found in China, Korea, and Japan, the raccoon dog has the least-sharp teeth of the canine family. It also plays dead to avoid predators and other natural enemies.

**COOKIECUTTER SHARK:** This small shark, infrequently seen by human eyes, has big lips and a belly that glows a pale blue-green color to help camouflage it from prey. Its name comes from the small, cookie-shaped bite marks it leaves.

**VAMPIRE SQUID:** This fast-moving gelatinous little squid has the largest eyes relative to its body of any animal in the world. Though it has no ink sack, with the aid of photophores it is able to light up its entire body. It is also able to invert itself, making it appear as if it's covered in suckers and sharp spikes.

**BLOBFISH:** Found lurking in the depths off the coasts of Australia and Tasmania, this strange-looking creature has been called the "most disgusting fish in the world." The blobfish does not have (nor need) muscles because its jellylike flesh is lighter than water, allowing it to simply float in the high-pressure areas of the ocean.

**PISTOL SHRIMP:** These striped crustaceans differ from other shrimp in that they have claws of differing sizes, one larger than the other. The pistol shrimp pulls back the larger claw and snaps it shut, producing a loud sound that stuns its prey. It has been said that the noise produced by a colony of these shrimp snapping their claws in unison is so loud it can block the sonar tracking of nearby submarines.

**SHOEBILL:** Discovered in the 19th century, this large bird is named for its beak, which is indeed shaped like a shoe. A long-legged, broad-winged relative of the stork, the shoebill stands four feet tall and has a seven-foot-wide wingspan. It also has a sharp hook on the end of its hefty beak, which is used for catching prey such as catfish.

**SUCKERFOOTED BAT:** A rare, diminutive bat, the suckerfoot is found in the western forests of Madagascar. It has small suction cups on its hands allowing them to cling to smooth surfaces as they glide through the forests in search of their next meal.

**THE YETI CRAB:** The pincers of this recently discovered crustacean from the depths of the South Pacific Ocean are covered in yellowish, bacteria-filled hair. Scientists hypothesize that the crabs possibly eat the bacteria, or perhaps use it to detoxify poisonous minerals.

**CHINESE GIANT SALAMANDER:** This particular salamander, found in the lakes and streams of China, is the world's largest living amphibian. Though its wrinkled appearance is similar to that of other salamanders, this variety can grow to over five feet in length, making it the undisputed king of salamanders.

**SHRIKE:** At first glance, this little bird seems gentle and charming; however, the shrike is infamous for catching and impaling its prey (usually insects, lizards, or small mammals) on thorns. This ultimately helps the bird tear its victims apart, for smaller, more manageable meals. The torn carcasses are then left on the thorns, so the shrike can return for later snacks.

**STAR-NOSED MOLE:** This lowland-living critter resembles a common mole, but with a nose that resembles a pink, many-armed starfish. Still, those weird nasal tentacles have nearly 100,000 minute touch receptors. Scientists have recently found that the star-nosed mole is also able to sniff underwater, by quickly inhaling the air bubbles that are blown out through its nostrils.

# ANIMALS THAT ARE EXTINCT BECAUSE OF HUMANS

## DODO
Probably the most famous species to have been eradicated by people, the dodo was a three-foot-tall flightless bird that lived on the island of Mauritius in the Indian Ocean. The dodo had no natural predators, so it was able to nest on the

ground in perfect safety until Dutch settlers arrived in the 16th century. Having never before been bothered, the dodo had no fear of people, nor of the sheep, dogs, pigs, and rats that accompanied them. The animals attacked the birds, the settlers destroyed their habitat, and the species disappeared in less than a century.

## EUROPEAN LION

Until the first century A.D., thousands of wild lions roamed modern-day Spain, Portugal, southern France, Italy, and the Balkans. This was the species pitted against the gladiators in Roman arenas. In addition to being slaughtered in amphitheaters, lions were hunted by the Macedonians and Greeks (among others), and it wasn't long before the Romans were forced to import lions from North Africa and the Middle East for their entertainment.

## PASSENGER PIGEON

At one point there were an estimated five billion passenger pigeons in the United States. They gathered in enormous flocks, sometimes consisting of as many as two billion birds. When European settlers began to colonize North America in the 17th century, they hunted the birds, mainly for food. By 1896, almost all of the flocks had been killed for sport by hunters, and in 1914, the last remaining passenger pigeon, known as Martha, died in the Cincinnati Zoo.

## BLUEBUCK OR BLUE ANTELOPE

This species of antelope lived on the southwestern coast of South Africa. It was widespread during the last ice age (though its numbers dwindled as the planet heated up again) and survived until the 17th century. Europeans began to hunt it obsessively—purely for sport, because they didn't like the taste of its meat—until it became extinct at the beginning of the 19th century.

## ALASKAN PREHISTORIC HORSE

Until recently, it was believed that these animals had died out because of climate changes long before the first people settled in Alaska. However, recent discoveries of fossil remains suggest that the horses may have been around when humans began to cross the Bering Land Bridge from Asia around 12,000 B.C. So it is likely that humankind had something to do with their extinction.

## GREAT AUK

Similar in appearance to the penguin, the flightless great auk was found in great numbers in eastern Canada, Greenland, Iceland, Norway, Ireland, and Great Britain. Although it couldn't use its wings to fly, the great auk used them to swim underwater, and its main food was fish. In the 18th century, great auks began to be hunted extensively for their meat and feathers, and they became extinct in 1844.

# Why Do Zebras Have Stripes?

The zebra is among the flashy few of the animal world. Like the butterfly, the tiger, and the peacock, the zebra looks like it treated itself to a vanity paint job. One of the theories explaining the evolutionary advantage of those flamboyant stripes sounds counter-intuitive: The stripes may actually help zebras blend in.

For one thing, vertical stripes can mesh with the vertical lines made by the tall grass that covers the ground in much of the zebra's natural habitat. There's a huge color difference, of course—tall grass comes in shades of yellow, green, and brown, which don't exactly match the stark black-and-white of the zebra's coat. But when it comes to effective camouflage, that might not matter so much, since the zebra's primary predators—lions and hyenas—seem to be colorblind.

The stripes may also give the zebras another way to visually confuse their predators. Zebras usually stick together in herds, where the clusters of vertical stripes can make it tricky for a predator to figure out where one zebra ends and another zebra begins. A lion, for example, might have difficulty honing in on any specific zebra, especially the more vulnerable foals. And once the herd starts to move, it's just a blur of stripes.

Some zoologists don't put much stock in the camouflage theory and suggest that the real evolutionary advantage of stripes has to do with zebra's social life. Every zebra has a unique stripe pattern, which could allow the animal to easily identify a friend (or perhaps a mortal enemy). Each zebra's stripe pattern serves as a sort of nametag, a way to be identified within a massive herd. Stripes may also help zebras stick together when predators attack, even at night. In case of emergency, zebra logic may say, follow the stripes.

Another theory suggests that zebra stripes are really a type of bug repellant. Tsetse flies, like other parasitic biting arthropods, seem to be drawn to large, one-colored surfaces—after all, that's what most large animals look like. But zebra stripes defy the norm, which may cause the tsetse flies to overlook the beasts when they're hunting for a free meal. There's strong evidence for this theory: First, tsetse flies bite zebras much less frequently than they bite other big animals nearby. Second, the regions of Africa where zebras sport more pronounced stripe patterns are also areas with bigger tsetse problems.

Of course, it's possible that the stripes may serve all of these purposes, at least to some degree. Or zebras might simply be showing off.

# FREAKY FACTS
# ABOUT ANIMAL MATING

- The funnel-web spider knocks his mate unconscious with pheromones before mating.

- The male *Argyrodes zonatus* spider secretes a drug that intoxicates the female, which is good because otherwise she would devour him.

- Harlequin bass and hamlet fish take turns being male and female, including releasing sperm and eggs during the mating process.

- Male North American fireflies flash their light every 5.8 seconds while females flash every 2 seconds, so there isn't any confusion.

- An albatross can spend weeks courting, and their relationships can last for decades. However, the actual act of mating lasts less than a minute.

- Fruit flies perform an elaborate seven-step dance before mating. If any part is not completed perfectly, there will be no copulation.

- Male mites mate with their sisters before they are born. After birth, the females rush off in search of food and their brothers are left to die.

- Mayflies live for one day, during which they do nothing but mate.

- The rattlesnake has two penises. The penis of the echidnas has four heads, and a pig's is shaped like a corkscrew.

- The male swamp antechinus, a mouselike marsupial in Australia, has sex until he dies, often from starvation. Sometimes he's simply too weak after mating to escape predators and is eaten.

# Why Does the Color Red Anger Bulls?

Red has been the color of choice of bullfighters for centuries. Their bright-red capes are used to incite their bovine opponents into spectacular rages. In fact, the phrase "seeing red" is believed to have originated from the fury that the color seems to provoke in the bull. What is it about red that ticks off bulls?

The truth is: nothing. Bulls are partially colorblind and don't respond to the color red at all. The red color of the cape is just eye candy for the audience, much like the bullfighter's *traje de luces* ("suit of lights").

Then is it the motion of the cape that infuriates the bull? The truth is: no. There's nothing that the matador does that makes the bull angry—it's in ill humor before it even enters the ring. These bulls aren't bred to take quiet walks in the park on Sunday afternoons. No, they are selected because they exhibit violent and aggressive behavior. By the time they hit the bullfighting arena, just about anything will set them off.

We're talking about bulls that have personalities like John McEnroe. The color red doesn't make them angry—everything makes them angry. Then again, the bullfighter plunging his sword into the bull's neck might have something to do with the beast's nasty disposition, too.

## How Do Worms Breathe?

Worms spend most of their lives underground, but they don't burrow in the traditional sense. Unlike most "underground" creatures, worms don't make tunnel systems and dens—instead, they squish, slide, and squirm through the soil, leaving nary a trace of their presence. Since they don't create any more room than they need for themselves in the earth, how is it possible for them to breathe? There can't be much air down there.

A worm lacks the accoutrements that are typically associated with breathing (i.e., a mouth, a nose, lungs). It breathes by taking in oxygen through the pores in its skin. To make this possible, the worm's skin must be moist. (This is why, after it rains, worms that are stranded on the sidewalk perish before they can get back into the soil—the sun dries them right out, suffocating them.) Oxygen is absorbed by the capillaries that line the surface of a worm's slimy skin; from there, it goes straight into the bloodstream. In mammals, this process is longer by one step: They take oxygen into their lungs, where it is then transferred to the bloodstream.

Worms can survive underwater for a sustained period of time, but their pores don't function the same way a fish's gills do, so a submerged worm will eventually drown. Some scientists believe that this is why worms come to the surface during a rainstorm: The soil becomes too wet and threatens to drown them. Of course, as we mentioned, this pilgrimage to the surface can lead to a different set of problems.

It seems that the key to a worm's longevity is to successfully squirm the fine line between too little and too much moisture. That, and avoiding the pinching fingers of anglers and curious kids.

# Why Are Skunks So Stinky?

Oh, so you smell like a bed of roses? But seriously, skunks have earned their odiferous reputation through their marvelous ability to make other things stink to high heaven.

All 11 species of skunk have stinky spray housed in their anal glands. However, as dog owners can attest, skunks aren't the only animals to have anal glands filled with terrible-smelling substances. Opossums are particularly bad stinkers; an opossum will empty its anal glands when "playing dead" to help it smell like a rotting corpse.

While no animal's anal glands are remotely fragrant, skunks' pack an especially pungent stench. This is because skunks use their spray as a defense mechanism. And they have amazing range: Skunks have strong muscles surrounding the glands, which allow them to spray 16 feet or more on a good day.

A skunk doesn't want to stink up the place. It does everything in its power to warn predators before it douses its target with *eau de skunk*. A skunk will jump up and down, stomp its feet, hiss, and lift its tail in the air, all in the hope that the predator will realize that it's dealing with a skunk and go away. A skunk only does what it does best when it feels it has no choice. Then it releases the nauseating mix of thiols (chemicals that contain super-stinky sulfur), which makes whatever it hits undateable for the foreseeable future. Skunks have enough "stink juice" stored up for about five or six sprays; after they empty their anal glands, it takes up to ten days to replenish the supply.

Being sprayed by a skunk is an extremely unpleasant experience. Besides the smell, the spray from a skunk can cause nausea and temporary blindness. Bobcats, foxes, coyotes, and badgers usually only hunt skunk if they are really, really hungry. Only the great horned owl makes skunk a regular snack—and the fact that the great horned owl barely has a sense of smell probably has a lot to do with it.

# Are There Cultures In Which Women Can Have Multiple Husbands?

When someone mentions polygamy, we usually think of certain Mormon fundamentalists or Muslim sects that allow a man to have multiple wives. Anthropologists use the term "polygamy" to refer to any marriage system that involves more than two people. The "one husband, many wives" form is called "polygyny." The "one wife, multiple husbands" version is called "polyandry." And if anthropologists have a special word for it, it must exist somewhere.

Polyandry is, however, exceedingly rare. Only a few cultures continue to practice it today, and polyandry is gradually being eroded by more modern ideas of love and marriage. The strongholds of polyandry are Tibet, Nepal, and certain parts of India, and it is also practiced in Sri Lanka. Other cultures were polyandrous in the past, though it was never widespread.

In many cases, this marriage practice takes the form of fraternal polyandry, in which one woman is married to several brothers. There may be a primary husband, the eldest brother or the first one she married. If additional brothers are born after the marriage, they usually become the woman's husbands as well.

The reasons for polyandry are typically more economic than religious. In the areas where it is practiced, life is difficult and poverty is rampant. If a family divided its property among all the brothers, no one would have enough land to survive on through farming and herding. Keeping all the brothers as part of one family keeps the familial plot in one piece. The herding lifestyle also means one or more brothers are often away tending the livestock for extended periods, so the other husbands can stay at home, protect the family, and tend the farm. Where resources are so limited, polyandry also serves as a form of birth control, since the wife can only get pregnant once every nine months no matter how many husbands she has. No one is ever sure which father sired which child, so each tends to treat all of the kids as if they are his own.

## CHEERS!

Raising glasses is a custom that occurs in countries around the world. Here are some of the many ways to toast.

*Cheers*—English, North America
*Ivjeli*—Croatian
*Fisehatak*—Arabic
*Prost*—German
*Salud*—used in many Latin countries, including Spain, Mexico, and Argentina
*Na zdorov´ya*—Bulgarian
*Gan bei*—Mandarin
*Pura vida*—Costa Rican
*Kippis*—Finnish
*À votre santé*—French
*Sláinte*—Irish (Gaelic)
*Yamas*—Grecian

*Okole maluna*—Hawaiian
*L´Chaim*—Hebrew
*Egészségedre*—Hungarian
*Pro*—Indonesian
*Kampai*—Japanese
*Chukbae*—Korean
*Saha wa´afiab*—Moroccan
*Skål*—Norwegian
*Sanda bashi*—Pakistani
*Na zdrowie*—Polish
*A sia saide*—Portugese
*Noroc*—Romanian
*Chtob vse bylizdorovy*—Russian
*Seiradewa*—Sri Lankan
*Afya*—Swahili
*Choc-tee*—Thai
*Budmo*—Ukranian

# What's Behind the Tradition of Flying Flags at Half-Mast?

As you might have guessed, the custom of flying a flag only midway up its pole has nautical roots. Lowering the colors to half-mast to symbolize mourning probably started in the 15th or 16th century, though no one knows precisely when. Nowadays, the gesture is recognized almost everywhere in the world—Europe, Asia, Africa, and the Americas.

The first historical mention of lowering a flag to recognize someone's death comes from the British Board of the Admiralty. In 1612, the British ship *Hearts Ease* searched for the elusive Northwest Passage, a sea route through the

Arctic Ocean connecting the Atlantic to the Pacific. During the voyage, Eskimos killed shipmaster James Hall. When the *Hearts Ease* sailed away to rejoin its sister ship, and again when it returned to London, its flag was lowered to trail over the stern as a sign of mourning.

That all who saw the *Hearts Ease* understood what the lowered flag meant suggests it was a common practice before then. Starting in 1660, ships of England's Royal Navy lowered their flags to half-mast each January 30, the anniversary of King Charles I's execution in 1649.

In the United States, the flag is to be flown at half-mast (or half-staff) on five designated days: Armed Forces Day (the third Saturday in May), Peace Officers Memorial Day (May 15), until noon on Memorial Day, Patriot Day (September 11), and Pearl Harbor Remembrance Day (December 7). In addition, according to the United States Code, the flag goes to half-mast for 30 days following the death of a U.S. president, past or present, and for 10 days following the death of the sitting vice president, a current or retired chief justice of the Supreme Court, or the speaker of the House.

For justices of the Supreme Court other than the chief justice, as well as for governors, former vice presidents, or cabinet secretaries of executive or military departments, the flag is lowered until the person is buried. For a member of Congress, the flag flies at half-mast for the day of and the day after the passing. By presidential order, the flag can also be lowered for the deaths of "principal figures" of the government or foreign dignitaries, such as the pope.

# THIS FESTIVAL EMBRACES "UNMENTIONABLE" HISTORY

Piqua, Ohio, sought a festival theme that would honor its past. Instead of honoring a local food or town founder, however, Piqua's answer was as close as, well, the underwear drawer.

Piqua has the dubious distinction of once having its major industry be the manufacture of unmentionables. The community's textile mills thrived, thanks in part to Piqua's convenient location along the Miami-Erie Canal. In fact, from the 1880s through the 1980s, as many as 15 different companies made underwear, long johns, and other knit undergarments.

## THE FABRIC OF THE TOWN

While earning the title "Underwear Capital of America" carries a certain honor, it also had some social consequence. During the late 1800s, the flourishing industry drove a wedge between residents who felt women should remain unemployed homemakers and those who supported a more liberated viewpoint. However, as women entered the workforce en masse, the cash flow that dual incomes brought on effectually ended the debate on women in the workplace.

The underwear business also changed the social fabric of Piqua, as women launched social clubs with like-minded female coworkers. The industry so permeated residents' lifestyles that future generations began to prepare for textile careers through high school classes.

In 1988, townspeople launched the Great Outdoor Underwear Festival as a way to celebrate Piqua's "unmentionable" history. The annual fall festival included events such as the Long John Parade, the Undy 500, the Boxer Ball, and the Drop-Seat Trot. Celebrities such as Pat Boone and Loni Anderson even donated their underwear for festival fund-raisers. Although the Great Outdoor Underwear Festival ceased in 1998, Piqua still beckons tourists with an impressive 23-block section of town that is listed on the National Register of Historic Places.

# 27 AMERICAN TERMS AND THEIR BRITISH EQUIVALENTS

## AMERICAN TERM—BRITISH TERM
1.  ballpoint pen—biro
2.  toilet paper—bog roll
3.  umbrella—brolly
4.  fanny pack—bum bag
5.  cotton candy—candy floss
6.  french fry—chip
7.  plastic wrap—clingfilm
8.  zucchini—courgette
9.  potato chip—crisp
10. checkers—draughts
11. thumbtack—drawing pin
12. busy signal—engaged tone
13. soccer—football
14. astonished—gobsmacked
15. sweater—jumper

16. elevator—lift
17. restroom—loo
18. truck—lorry
19. ground beef—mince
20. diaper—nappy
21. mailbox—pillar box
22. bandage (Band-Aid)—plaster
23. baby carriage/stroller—pram
24. collect call—reverse-charge call
25. aluminum can—tin
26. to go drastically wrong—to go pear-shaped
27. complain—whinge

# Why Did Ancient Egyptians Shave Their Eyebrows?

Shaving away all bodily hair, including eyebrows, was part of an elaborate daily purification ritual practiced by Pharaoh and his priests.

The ancient Egyptians believed that everything in their lives—health, good crops, victory, prosperity—depended on keeping their gods happy, so one of Pharaoh's duties was to enter a shrine and approach a special statue of a god three times a day, every day. Each time he visited the shrine, Pharaoh washed the statue, anointed it with oil, and dressed it in fresh linen. Because Pharaoh was a busy guy, high-ranking priests often performed this duty for him. But whether it was Pharaoh or a priest doing it, he had to bathe himself and shave his eyebrows beforehand.

Shaving the eyebrows was also a sign of mourning, even among commoners. The Greek historian Herodotus, who traveled and wrote in the 5th century B.C., said that everyone in an ancient Egyptian household would shave his or her eyebrows following the natural death of a pet cat. For dogs, he reported, the household members would shave their heads and all of their body hair as well.

Herodotus was known to repeat some wild stories in his books—for instance, that serpents with bat-like wings flew from Arabia into Egypt and were killed in large numbers by ibises. Herodotus claimed he actually saw heaps of these serpent skeletons. So you might want to take his eyebrow-shaving claim with a grain of salt...and a pinch of catnip.

# Why Is a White Flag a Symbol of Surrender?

It seems like a cliché straight out of a 1950s B-movie or an episode of *Hogan's Heroes*. Despondent and fearing for their lives, the vanquished search desperately for anything white—a handkerchief, a shirt, a pair of underpants—and attach it to a stick. They then proceed cautiously (or, in the case of *Hogan's Heroes*, clumsily) toward their gloating foe.

In reality, the tradition of the white flag as a symbol of surrender or truce goes back a couple of thousand years. In the West, the Roman historian Tacitus mentioned a white flag of surrender that was used at the Second Battle of Cremona in A.D. 69. In the East, the use of a white surrender flag is believed to date back just as distantly.

It's unclear how the color white first came to symbolize surrender. Flag experts surmise that it happened because white is a neutral hue, one that could be easily distinguished from the colorful banners that armies often carried into battle. Today, the use of the white flag as a sign of peace or surrender is an official part of the rules of warfare, as referenced in the Geneva Conventions.

The white flag has had other military uses throughout history, though none lasted long. For a short time during the Civil War, the Confederacy used a mostly white national flag that was known as the "Stainless Banner"—however, it caused confusion in battle and was scrapped. During the 1600s, the French (those lovable contrarians) used a white flag to signify the intent to go to battle. Historians don't tell us whether the French looked with disdain at anyone who didn't understand their unconventional use of the white flag—but we can guess that they did.

# THE ORIGIN OF INDOOR PLUMBING

The luxury of a "civilized" life would not be possible without water pipes.

Humble hollow tubes have been improving our quality of life for thousands of years. As it turns out, the piping of water in and out of living spaces originated in many different ancient civilizations. Plumbing technology was often developed only to be lost until it was reinvented from scratch. Lead pipes have been found in Mesopotamian ruins, and clay knee joint piping has been traced to Babylonia. The Egyptians used copper piping. But the most sophisticated ancient waterworks flourished at the hands of the Harappan Civilization (circa 3300–1600 B.C.) in the areas of present-day India and Pakistan.

The Harappans boasted of a network of earthenware pipes that would carry water from people's homes into municipal drains and cesspools. Archeological excavation in the 1920s uncovered highly planned cities with living quarters featuring individual indoor baths and even toilets. Thanks to the Harappans' advanced ceramic techniques, they were able to build ritual baths up to 29 feet long and 10 feet deep—as big as modern-day swimming pools.

While the Romans can't be credited with the invention of water pipes, their mastery of pipe-making influenced plumbing up to the 20th century. (The word plumbing comes from the Latin word for lead, *plumbum*.) Pipes were made by shaping sheets of the easily malleable (and highly toxic) molten lead around a wooden core. Plumbers then soldered the joints together with hot lead. It could be said that they were largely responsible for "civilizing" Rome, making it a place where homes had bathtubs as well as indoor toilets that flushed into underground sewage systems. Fresh water was piped directly into kitchens, and there were even ways of "metering" how much water was being used by the width of the pipe installed. (Even then, convenience had its price!)

# FOREIGN SLANG TERMS

English borrows freely from nearly every language it comes into contact with. However, there are still many concepts and situations for which Anglophones still lack *le mot juste*.

Here are some suggested foreign words to add to the English dictionary.

**Backpfeifengesicht (German):** a face that's just begging for someone to slap it—a familiar concept to anyone fond of daytime TV.

**Bakku-shan (Japanese):** a girl who looks pretty from the back but not the front. This loanword would in fact be a loanword regifted, since it's already a combination of the English word "back" with the German word *schoen*, meaning "beautiful."

**Kummerspeck (German):** literally this means "grief bacon": excess weight gained from overeating during emotionally trying times.

**Ølfrygt (Viking Danish):** the fear of a lack of beer. Often sets in during trips away from one's hometown, with its familiar watering holes.

**Drachenfutter (German):** literally "dragon fodder": a makeup gift bought in advance. Traditionally used to denote offerings made by a man to his wife when he knows he's guilty of something.

**Bol (Mayan):** For the Mayans of South Mexico and Honduras, the word *bol* pulls double duty, meaning both "in-laws" as well as "stupidity."

**Uitwaaien (Dutch):** walking in windy weather for the sheer fun of it.

**Blechlawine (German):** literally "sheet metal avalanche": the endless lineup of cars stuck in a traffic jam on the highway.

**Karelu (Tulu, south of India):** the mark left on the skin by wearing anything tight.

# THE SECRET ORIGIN OF COMIC BOOKS

Today's graphic novels have a long history that stretches back to newspaper comic strips.

In the 1920s and '30s, comic strips were among the most popular sections of newspapers and were often reprinted later in book form. Generally, these were inexpensive publications that looked like newspaper supplements, though other formats were tried (including "big little books" in which the comic panels were adapted and text was added opposite each panel).

These so-called "funny books" were often given away as premiums for products such as cereal, shoes, and even gasoline. Then, in 1933, a sales manager at the Eastern Color Printing Company in Waterbury, Connecticut, hit on a winning format: 36 pages of color comics in a size similar to modern comics. *Famous Funnies: A Carnival of Comics*, considered the first true comic book, featured reprinted strips from such comics as *Mutt and Jeff*. It was still a giveaway, but it was a hit. The next year, Eastern Color published *Famous Funnies #1* and distributed the 68-page comic book to newsstands nationwide with a cover price of 10 cents.

As the demand for reprinted strips outpaced supply,

publishers began introducing original material into comic books. One publisher, searching for features to fill the pages of a new book, approached a young creative team made up of writer Jerry Siegel and artist Joe Shuster, who had been trying for years to sell a newspaper strip about an invincible hero from another planet. Siegel and Shuster reformatted the strips into comic book form, and Superman debuted in *Action Comics #1*. It was an instant smash hit. The "Golden Age" of comics followed, introducing many of the popular heroes who are still with us today, including Batman, Wonder Woman, Captain America, and The Flash. In the 1960s, the "Silver Age" introduced new, more emotionally flawed heroes such as Spider-Man, Iron Man, and the Hulk. The comic book has certainly come a long way since *Mutt and Jeff*.

# WHAT'S IN A PHRASE?

## BLUE BLOODS
In the Middle Ages, the veins of the fair-complexioned people of Spain appeared blue. To distinguish them as untainted by the Moors, they referred to themselves as blue-blooded.

## ROB PETER TO PAY PAUL
In the mid-1550s, estates in St. Peter's, Westminster, were appropriated to pay for the new St. Paul's Cathedral. This process revived a phrase that preacher John Wycliffe had used 170 years before in *Select English Works*.

## HUMBLE PIE
While medieval lords and ladies dined on the finest foods, servants had to utilize leftovers (the "umbles," or offal) when

preparing their meals. To eat humble pie means to exercise humility or self-effacement.

## MEN OF STRAW

In medieval times, men would hang around English courts of law, eager to be hired as false witnesses. They identified themselves with a straw in their shoe.

## WHITE ELEPHANT

Once upon a time in Siam, rare albino elephants were to receive nothing but the best from their owners. Therefore, no one wanted to own one.

## TOUCH AND GO

English ships in the 18th century would often hit bottom in shallow water, only to be released with the next wave. The phrase indicated that they had narrowly averted danger.

## BY HOOK OR BY CROOK

This phrase describes a feudal custom that allowed tenants to gather as much wood from their lord's land as they could rake from the undergrowth or pull down from the trees with a crook.

# UNUSUAL WORLD CUSTOMS

## TABLE MANNERS

- In Italy, eat spaghetti as the Romans do—with a fork only. Using a spoon to help collect the pasta is considered uncouth.

- It is considered improper and impolite to use silverware to eat chicken in Turkey.

- Keep your right elbow off the table when eating in Chile. (Just be sure not to elbow your neighbor.)

- In the United States, one should never butter an entire piece of bread before eating it. The proper, if impractical, way to eat bread is to pull off a small bit from your larger piece and butter it before popping it into your mouth.

- In China, slurping one's food and belching at the end of the meal are considered acceptable and even polite.

- Tipping is uncommon, and even considered rude, in many Asian countries.

## PERSONAL CARE

- Up until the 19th century, long fingernails were considered a symbol of gentility and wealth among the Chinese aristocracy. Wealthy Chinese often sported fingernails several inches in length and protected them by wearing special coverings made of gold.

- In ancient Rome, urine was commonly used as a tooth whitener.

- In many countries, toilet paper is unheard of. Instead, people wash themselves after using the bathroom, using their left hand. For this reason it is considered rude to use the left hand in many social situations.

## BODY LANGUAGE

- In Chile, pounding your left palm with your right fist is considered vulgar.

- In Thailand, feet are considered unclean. Using one's foot to move an object or gesture toward somebody is considered the height of rudeness. Similarly, one should never cross their legs when in the presence of elders.

- When conversing in Quebec, keep your hands where they can be seen. Talking with your hands in your pockets is considered rude.

- Make sure to get enough sleep when traveling through Ecuador. Yawning in public is considered tacky.

## HOLIDAYS

- The people of Ottery St. Mary, England, celebrate Guy Fawkes Day by racing through the streets of their town with barrels of flaming tar strapped to their backs.

- In many Latin American cultures, a girl's 15th birthday is considered one of the most important days of her life. Known as the quinceanera, the celebration can be as elaborate as a wedding.

- In Sweden, the Christmas season begins on Santa Lucia's Day (December 13), when the eldest daughter of a household, clad in white and wearing a wreath with seven lit candles on her head, serves her family breakfast in bed.

## RITUALS AND TRADITIONS

- Until being banned in 1912, foot binding was common in China. The practice, which involved breaking girls' toes and wrapping them tightly in cloth, prevented women's feet from growing normally. Small, dainty feet were considered a symbol of status.

- In parts of India, some women still perform *sati*, an ancient custom in which a widow throws herself on the funeral pyre of her deceased husband to commit suicide.

- For almost 500 years, a form of conflict resolution known as "dueling" took place in Western Europe and the United States. The highly ritualistic tradition began with the offended party throwing down his glove at the foot of another and ended with a sword or pistol fight—often to the death.

- In parts of Tibet, some people practice a funeral ritual known as a "sky burial." In this ceremony, the body of the deceased is dissected and placed atop a mountain as an offering to the elements and birds of prey.

# Where Does the Term "Shanghaied" Come From?

From California, according to the Reverend William Taylor. A Methodist minister who spent his life traveling and preaching, Taylor wrote a book in 1856 about his years in San Francisco spent preaching to destitute men. He defined "shanghaied" as the act of drugging men and forcing them to serve on sailing ships.

Taylor came to San Francisco during California's gold rush in the mid-1800s and found a city of disillusioned men and abandoned ships. Hundreds of vessels sailed into San Francisco, but few sailed out because crew members jumped ship to search for gold. That left ships with undelivered cargo. If a crew—willing or unwilling—could be found, those ships could sail and make money. So men were forced onto the ships—in other words, they were shanghaied.

Why was the practice referred to as shanghaied? According to the men Taylor met, going anywhere by way of Shanghai, China, meant taking the longest route possible—and a shanghaied man faced a long passage home. The word caught on and for decades was used to describe the kidnapping and forced labor of sailors, even though many of these men likely never went anywhere near Shanghai.

An entire business hierarchy arose in the 1800s to get crews for sailing ships. Men called crimps would use drugs, alcohol, or weapons such as blackjacks to render a subject unconscious. The victim would awaken at sea. The ship's captain had paid the crimp the equivalent of a sailor's wages for a month or two, and the shanghaied soul had to work off that money. Months, even years, might pass before he again saw home.

The attacks occurred in dark, crime-ridden areas or shabby boardinghouses, and the victims were unable to appeal to authorities until they returned from sea. The shanghaied were usually poor, alone, and illiterate. Few had the means to hire a lawyer or press charges. And police and city officials were often bribed to turn blind eyes to such practices.

Although the term originated in San Francisco, the practice of shanghaiing sailors was carried out by crimps and their accomplices in ports all over North America: New York; Boston; Philadelphia; Baltimore; Tacoma and Port Townsend in Washington; Portland, Oregon; Galveston, Texas; New Orleans; Savannah, Georgia; and Mobile, Alabama. Experts guess that from the 1860s to 1910, a large percentage of the sailors on merchant ships were shanghaied.

Kidnapping men for forced labor at sea was outlawed by Congress in 1906. The new law set a fine of up to one thousand dollars or a prison term, or both, for convicted crimps. The Seaman's Act of 1915 added a prohibition against prepaying a sailor's wages to crimps. With no profits to be made, the custom ended.

The term shanghaied remains in use, but its meaning has mellowed. Nowadays, if you are shanghaied, it means you've been tricked or "volunteered" into some unpopular duty, like driving Grandma to the airport.

# THE START OF MANY THINGS

These intriguing stories offer insight into the history of some everyday items, expressions, and endeavors—stuff you never think to think about.

## THE LATIN ALPHABET

People had been writing hieroglyphics (symbols that stood for objects such as dog, reed, or pyramid) for at least a millennium before the first glimmer of an actual alphabet appeared. Around 2000 B.C., a group of Egyptian slaves (the Semitics) figured out how to communicate with one another using symbols that represented sounds, not just things. From this system, we eventually got the Phoenician and Aramaic alphabets, as well as the Greek and Latin alphabets. Early Greek was written right to left, before the "ox-turning" method (in which the direction of writing changed with every line) was adopted. By the 5th century B.C., the left-to-right method was in place.

## THE FACE-LIFT

Contrary to popular belief, the "plastic" in "plastic surgery" doesn't refer to the use of petroleum-based materials; rather, it's from the Greek word *plastikos*, meaning "to mold or shape." The first facial plastic surgeries date back to ancient Rome, when they were probably performed to fix ears and noses that had been torn off during Coliseum scuffles. It wasn't until the 1900s that face-lifts, or *rhytidectomies* (literally, the surgical removal of wrinkles), were performed for cosmetic reasons. These days, plastic surgeons in the United States snip and pull the skin on men and women's faces at the rate of approximately 150,000 a year.

## THE JUMP ROPE

Skipping and jumping are natural movements of the body (especially for kids), and the inclusion of a rope in these activities dates back to A.D. 1600, when Egyptian children jumped over vines. Early Dutch settlers brought the game to North America, where it flourished and evolved from a simple motion into the often elaborate form prevalent today: double Dutch. With two people turning two ropes simultaneously, a third, and then fourth, person jumps in, often reciting rhymes. Jumping techniques have become so complex that there are now worldwide organizations that sponsor double Dutch competitions.

## TAXICABS

Think of Cleopatra being carted around on a sedan chair, and you have the origins of the modern-day taxicab. Rickshaws replaced sedan chairs as a means of transporting people from one place to another, followed by horse-drawn carriages, which finally gave us poor humans a rest. At the end of the 19th century, automobiles started to fill the streets, and with the invention of the taximeter (an instrument that measures both the time and distance a vehicle has traveled), transport by cab became increasingly popular.

# Is It True That Eskimos Have a Thousand Words For Snow?

It stands to reason that the Eskimos would have a lot of words for snow. Their lives revolve around the stuff, after all. But it seems that reports of the exact number of words have, well, snowballed.

There are five major Eskimo languages. The most widely used is Inuit, which is spoken by people living in northern Alaska, Canada, and Greenland. The notion that Eskimos have lots of words for snow started with anthropologist Frank Boas, who spent much of the late 19th century living with Eskimos in British Columbia and on Baffin Island of Upper Canada. He wrote in the introduction to his 1911 book *Handbook of North American Indians* that the Inuit language alone had four words for snow: *aput* ("snow on the ground"), *qana* ("falling snow"), *piqsirpoq* ("drifting snow"), and *qimuqsoq* ("a snowdrift").

Boas believed that differences in cultures were reflected in differences in language structure and usage. This wasn't to say that Inuits saw snow differently, according to Boas, but that they organized their thinking and their vocabulary about snow in a more complex manner because snow was such a big part of their daily life.

In 1940, anthropologist Benjamin Whorf claimed the Eskimo/ Inuit language contained seven words for snow. In 1984, Steven Jacobson published the *Yup'ik Eskimo Dictionary*, which placed the figure for the Yup'ik Eskimos at well into the hundreds. Exaggeration piles upon exaggeration, and pretty soon a thousand words for snow sounds reasonable.

In a July 1991 article critiquing Jacobson's dictionary, University of Texas linguist Anthony Woodbury claimed the problem is lexemes. Lexemes are individual units of meaning: For example, the word "speak" can be transformed into the words spoken, speech, speaking, spoke, and so on. Woodbury noted that noun lexemes in at least one of the Eskimo languages can be arranged into more than 250 different individual words or phrases, and verbs allow for even more differentiations. He claimed that there were only 15 individual lexemes for snow shared among the five Eskimo languages. That's not all that different from the English language.

# HAPPY BIRTHDAY, DEAR VALENTINE?

Why do we celebrate St. Valentine's birthday? We don't. Instead, we commemorate his martyrdom.

Who was St. Valentine? The Catholic Church says there were actually three St. Valentines, and all were martyrs. So which one does Valentine's Day honor? The most likely candidate was a Roman priest during the reign of Claudius II, emperor of Rome from A.D. 268 to 270. Desperate for men to fight his wars, Claudius forbade soldiers to marry. According to the legend, young lovers came to Valentine to be married, and these unauthorized marriages led to his imprisonment. While awaiting his execution, he fell in love with his jailer's daughter. Shortly before his death on February 14, he wrote her a letter and signed it "From Your Valentine."

The problem is that there's no proof that any of this actually happened. Valentine's name is not on the earliest list of Roman martyrs, and there's no evidence that he was put to death on February 14. In fact, in 1969, the Catholic Church removed Valentine's Day from the list of official holy days.

How did Valentine become associated with a celebration of love? It may be that February 14 was chosen by the early Church to replace a Roman fertility festival called Lupercalia, which fell on the same date. Another explanation is that the sentimentality of Valentine's Day can be traced to the Middle Ages, an era fixated on romantic love. It was popularly believed that birds chose their mates on February 14, a legend Geoffrey Chaucer referenced in his poem "Parliament of Foules": "For this was on St. Valentine's Day, when every fowl cometh there to chooses his mate."

What about all the flowers and chocolates? These fairly recent additions to the Valentine story have more to do with the power of retailers than the passion of romance.

# ODD SPORTING EVENTS AROUND THE WORLD

## CHEESE ROLLING

If you're a whiz at cheese rolling, you may want to head to Brockworth in Gloucestershire, England, at the annual Cooper's Hill Cheese Roll held each May. The ancient festival dates back hundreds of years and involves pushing and shoving a large, mellow, seven- to eight-pound wheel of ripe Gloucestershire cheese downhill in a race to the bottom. With the wheels of cheese reaching up to 70 miles per hour, runners chase, tumble, and slide down the hill after their cheese but don't usually catch up until the end. The winner gets to take home his or her cheese, while the runners-up get cash prizes.

## TOE WRESTLING

This little piggy went to the World Toe Wrestling Championship held annually in July in Derbyshire, England. Contestants sit facing each other at a "toedium"—a stadium for toes—and try to push each other's bare foot off a small stand called a "toesrack." Three-time champion Paul Beech calls himself the "Toeminator." Toe wrestling began in the town of Wetton in 1970, and the international sport is governed by the World Toe Wrestling Organization, which once applied for Olympic status but was rejected.

## TUNA THROWING

Popular in Australia, tuna throwing requires contestants to whirl a frozen tuna around their heads with a rope and then fling it like an Olympic hammer thrower. Since 1998, the record holder has been former Olympic hammer thrower Sean Carlin, with a tuna toss of 122 feet. With $7,000 in prize money overall, the event is part of Tunarama, an annual festival held in late January in Port Lincoln, South Australia. Animal rights activists will be pleased to know that the tuna are spoiled fish that stores refused to sell.

## POOH STICKS

Christopher Robin knows that pooh sticks is not a hygiene problem but rather a game played with Winnie the Pooh. The game consists of finding a stick, dropping it into a river, and then seeing how long it takes to get to the finish line. There is even an annual World Pooh Sticks Championship held in mid-March in Oxfordshire, England. Individual event winners receive gold, silver, and bronze medals, and a team event has attracted competitors from Japan, Latvia, and the Czech Republic.

## MAN VERSUS HORSE MARATHON

The Man Versus Horse Marathon is an annual race between humans and horse-and-rider teams held in early June in the Welsh town of Llanwrtyd Wells. The event started in 1980 when a pub keeper overheard two men debating which was faster in a long race—man or horse. Slightly shorter than a traditional marathon, the 22-mile course is filled with many natural obstacles, and horses win nearly every year. But in 2004, Huw Lobb made history as the first runner to win the race (in 2 hours, 5 minutes, and 19 seconds), taking the £25,000 (about $47,500) prize, which was the accumulation of 25 yearly £1,000 prizes that had not been claimed. Apparently, the horse doesn't get to keep its winnings.

# BULL RUNNING

While bullfighting is popular in many countries, the sport of bull running—which should really be called bull outrunning—is pretty much owned by Pamplona, Spain. The event dates back to the 13th and 14th centuries as a combination of festivals honoring St. Fermin and bullfighting. Every morning for a week in July, the half-mile race is on between six bulls and hundreds of people. Most of the participants try to get as close to the bulls as possible, and many think it's good luck to touch one.

# TOMATO TOSSING

Tomatoes aren't just for salads and sauce anymore. La Tomatina is a festival held in late August in the small town of Buñol, Spain, where approximately 30,000 people come from all over the world to pelt one another with nearly 140 tons of overripe tomatoes. The fruit fight dates back to the mid-1940s but was banned under Francisco Franco, then returned in the 1970s after his death. After two hours of tomato-tossing at La Tomatina, there are no winners or losers, only stains and sauce, and the cleanup begins.

# HUMAN TOWER BUILDING

If you enjoy watching cheerleaders form human pyramids, you'll love the castellers, people who compete to form giant human towers at festivals around Catalonia, Spain. Castellers form a solid foundation of packed bodies, linking arms and hands together in an intricate way that holds several tons and softens the fall in case the tower collapses, which is not uncommon. Up to eight more levels of people are built, each layer standing on the shoulders of the people below. The top levels are made up of children and when complete, the castell resembles a human Leaning Tower of Pisa.

## WIFE CARRYING CHAMPIONSHIP

During the Wife Carrying Championship, held annually in Sonkajärvi, Finland, contestants carry a woman—it needn't be their wife—over an 832-foot course with various obstacles en route. Dropping the woman incurs a 15-second penalty, and the first team to reach the finish line receives the grand prize—the weight of the "wife" in beer! This bizarre event traces its origins to the 19th century when a local gang of bandits commonly stole women from neighboring villages.

# WACKY SPORTS INJURIES

**Ryan Klesko**—In 2004, this San Diego Padre was in the middle of pregame stretches when he jumped up for the singing of the national anthem and pulled an oblique/rib-cage muscle, which sidelined him for more than a week.

**Freddie Fitzsimmons**—In 1927, New York Giants pitcher "Fat Freddie" Fitzsimmons was napping in a rocking chair when his pitching hand got caught under the chair and was crushed by his substantial girth. Surprisingly, he only missed three weeks of the season.

**Clarence "Climax" Blethen**—Blethen wore false teeth, but he believed he looked more intimidating without them. During a 1923 game, the Red Sox pitcher had the teeth in his back pocket when he slid into second base. The chompers bit his backside and he had to be taken out of the game.

**Chris Hanson**—During a publicity stunt for the Jacksonville Jaguars in 2003, a tree stump and ax were placed in the locker room to remind players to "keep chopping wood," or give it their all. Punter Chris Hanson took a swing and missed the stump, sinking the ax into his non-kicking foot. He missed the remainder of the season.

**Lionel Simmons**—As a rookie for the Sacramento Kings, Simmons devoted hours to playing his Nintendo Game Boy. In fact, he spent so much time playing the video game system that he missed a series of games during the 1991 season due to tendonitis in his right wrist.

**Jaromir Jagr**—During a 2006 playoff game, New York Ranger Jagr threw a punch at an opposing player. Jagr missed, his fist slicing through the air so hard that he dislocated his shoulder. After the Rangers were eliminated from the playoffs, Jagr underwent surgery and continued his therapy during the next season.

**Paulo Diogo**—After assisting on a goal in a 2004 match, newlywed soccer player Diogo celebrated by jumping up on a perimeter fence, accidentally catching his wedding ring on the wire. When he jumped down he tore off his finger. To make matters worse, the referee issued him a violation for excessive celebration.

**Clint Barmes**—Rookie shortstop Barmes was sidelined from the Colorado Rockies lineup for nearly three months in 2005 after he broke his collarbone when he fell carrying a slab of deer meat.

**Darren Barnard**—In the late 1990s, professional British soccer player Barnard was sidelined for five months with knee ligament damage after he slipped in a puddle of his puppy's pee on the kitchen floor. The incident earned him the unfortunate nickname "Whiz Kid."

**Marty Cordova**—A fan of the bronzed look, Cordova was a frequent user of tanning beds. However, he once fell asleep while catching some rays, resulting in major burns to his face and body that forced him to miss several games with the Baltimore Orioles.

**Gus Frerotte**—In 1997, Washington Redskins quarterback Frerotte had to be taken to the hospital and treated for a concussion after he spiked the football and slammed his head into a foam-covered concrete wall while celebrating a touchdown.

**Jamie Ainscough**—A rough and ready rugby player from Australia, Ainscough's arm became infected in 2002, and doctors feared they might need to amputate. But after closer inspection, physicians found the source of the infection—the tooth of a rugby opponent had become lodged under his skin, unbeknownst to Ainscough who had continued to play for weeks after the injury.

**Sammy Sosa**—In May 2004, Sosa sneezed so hard that he injured his back, sidelining the Chicago Cubs all-star outfielder and precipitating one of the worst hitting slumps of his career.

# Why Does K Stand for Strikeout?

To the uninitiated, a baseball scorecard can look like hieroglyphs in need of the Rosetta stone: numbers, circles, lines, colored diamonds, and more abbreviations than an IM conversation between teens. And when the seven-dollar beers start flowing in the grandstand—forget about it.

Actually, most of these abbreviations are fairly easy to decipher. It doesn't take a sabermetrician to figure out that HR stands for "home run" and BB stands for "base on balls." But what genius designated K the symbol for strikeout?

That would be Henry Chadwick, writer, National Baseball Hall of Fame member, and inventor of the baseball box score. Chadwick was born in England in 1824 and grew up an avid fan of the English ball games cricket and rounders. He emigrated to the United States as a young man, and in the 1850s, as the relatively new sport of baseball gained popularity in America, Chadwick became a devoted fan. Chadwick at the time was a newspaper reporter in New York, and at his urging the city's major newspapers added coverage of baseball games to their agendas.

A lot happens in a baseball game, and Chadwick knew it wasn't always easy to keep track of what was going on—especially when the thirteen-cent beers started flowing in the grandstand. In 1861, in a treatise curiously titled *Beadle's Dime Base-Ball Player*, Chadwick introduced a scorecard for baseball games. It was adapted from one used by reporters to keep track of cricket matches.

Chadwick's early scorecard was an unwieldy, Excel-worthy spreadsheet. It involved 29 columns 13 rows deep, and provided space for stats of the day like "bounds" and "muffs." It also included space to record what happened on a play-to-play basis, all the better to recreate the game in tomorrow morning's newspaper.

Because S was so common in baseball's statistical lexicon ("stolen base," "sacrifice," "strikeout"), Chadwick chose K to represent the whiff. Why K? It's the last letter in "struck," which was the common term used to describe the strikeout in the 1860s.

The baseball scorecard has grown more usable and comprehensible over the years, but much of Chadwick's original form and symbolism survives, including the use of K for a strikeout. Nowadays, many fans take it further by using a normal K to represent a swinging strikeout and a backward K to represent a called third strike.

Chadwick, who devoted his life to promoting baseball, would no doubt delight at the immense popularity the game attained. It's doubtful he'd be impressed by the beer sales, however. He was a strong supporter of the temperance movement.

# BIGGEST SOCCER RIOTS OF ALL TIME

Despite its lack of popularity in the United States, soccer is by far the most popular sport worldwide. Only slightly less popular, though, is the less skilled sport of "soccer rioting"— also known as hooliganism. Here are some of the biggest riots in soccer history.

## LIMA, PERU: MAY 24, 1964
This one was a doozy. During an Olympic qualifying match between Peru and Argentina, frenzied Peruvian fans grew irate when referees disallowed a goal for the home team. The resulting riot left 300 people dead and 500 injured.

## CALCUTTA, INDIA: AUGUST 16, 1980

Tensions were already high in post-partition India when an official's call sparked rioting during a soccer match in Calcutta. The result: 16 dead, 100 injured.

## BRUSSELS, BELGIUM: MAY 29, 1985

Nobody does soccer riots like the British, who are so good they can cause riots in other countries. Take the case of the "Heysel Disaster"—a match in Brussels between British team Liverpool and Italian club Juventus. The game hadn't even begun when a crowd of drunk Liverpool supporters charged toward a group of Juventus fans. The stampede caused a stadium wall to collapse, resulting in 39 deaths and a five-year ban on all British soccer teams in Europe.

## ZAGREB, CROATIA: MAY 13, 1990

In a grim harbinger of the ethnic violence that would ensnare the region over the next few years, Serbs and Croats fought each other before, during, and after a match between the Dinamo Zagreb and the Red Star Belgrade soccer teams, leaving hundreds wounded and throwing the city into a state of chaos.

## ORKNEY, SOUTH AFRICA: JANUARY 13, 1991

Fights broke out in the grandstand during a game between the Kaizer Chiefs and Orlando Pirates after a disputed goal. In the ensuing rush of panicked fans trying to flee the fights, more than 40 people were killed and another 50 were injured. Ironically, most of the deaths were a result of being crushed against riot-control fencing. Fans of these two teams would combine for another riot in 2001, in which 43 people were killed.

## ACCRA, GHANA: MAY 9, 2001

Unruly fans throwing bottles and chairs onto the field during a Ghanaian soccer match were bad enough, but to make it worse, police responded by firing tear gas into the jammed grandstands. The resulting panic killed more than 100 people.

## MOSCOW, RUSSIA: JUNE 9, 2002

When Russia lost to Japan in the 2002 World Cup, Russian fans decided to express their disappointment by setting fire to Moscow. The ensuing riots left one dead and more than two dozen injured, including a group of Japanese tourists.

## BASEL, SWITZERLAND: MAY 13, 2006

The Swiss might be neutral when it comes to wars, but they certainly are passionate about their football. Never was this more apparent than when FC Basel lost their chance to win the Swiss League title when FC Zurich scored a late goal in their match. The resulting riot—which included fans storming the field and attacking FC Zurich's players—resulted in more than 100 injuries and became known as the "Disgrace of Basel."

## MANCHESTER, ENGLAND: MAY 2008

Observers knew there was going to be trouble when hooligans began fighting the day before the 2008 UEFA Cup Final. But the rioters kicked it up a notch on game day, attacking police officers and lighting things on fire in a sad display that became known as the "Battle of Piccadilly." The impetus? The failure of a large television screen erected to give fans without tickets a view of the game.

# THE LOWDOWN ON HOCKEY FIGHTS

The old joke is, "I went to a fight and a hockey game broke out." A typical pro football game has regular skirmishes, and major league baseball teams clear the benches to brawl over a hangnail. And people call hockey ultraviolent?

You've heard it before: "I love hockey! It's the only team sport that allows fighting." In fact, it doesn't. Hockey measures penalties in minutes: two-minute minors, five-minute majors, ten-minute misconducts, and ejection for a game misconduct or match penalty. Fighting is a five-minute major penalty.

## CAN'T YOU PLAY NICE?

Let's compare some of the other hockey crimes, many of which merit less sin-bin time than fighting. You can't shove with the shaft of the stick, hook someone with it, or slash with it like a broadsword. These minor penalties usually merit only two minutes in the hockey hoosegow. Major penalties besides fighting include stabbing with the stick's blade or butt, ramming someone too hard into the boards (how subjective is that?), and any flagrant version of a minor penalty (e.g., you shove someone aside with the stick shaft in his face).

## THAT'S SOME SPORT

If you join a fight in progress or get your third fighting major in the game, you'll be charged with automatic game misconduct. Breaking your stick in frustration, grossly disrespecting officials, and flipping the bird or a puck at the fans: misconduct. Leaving the penalty box early: game misconduct. Pulling hair: match penalty. You can also get the heave-ho for kicking with your skate blade, spitting on someone, head-butting, throwing the stick like a javelin, face-masking, biting, or any act seen as a deliberate attempt to injure. On second thought, maybe the game is ultraviolent.

# How Do Corked Bats Help Baseball Players Hit Farther?

In this age of performance-enhancing drugs, it's almost refreshing when a hitter gets caught cheating the old-fashioned way. Corked bats somehow recall a more innocent time.

There are different ways to cork a wooden baseball bat, but the basic procedure goes like this: Drill a hole into the top of the bat, about an inch in diameter and 12 inches deep; fill the hole with cork—in rolled sheets or ground up—and close the top with a wooden plug that matches the bat; finally, stain and finish the top of the bat so that the plug blends in.

The supposed benefits of a corked bat involve weight and bat speed. Cork is lighter than wood, which enables a player to generate more speed when swinging the bat. The quicker the swing, the greater the force upon contact with the ball—and the farther that ball flies. The lighter weight allows a batter more time to evaluate a pitch, since he can make up the difference with his quicker swing; this extra time amounts to only a fraction of a second, but it can be the difference between a hit and an out at the major league level.

Following the logic we've set forth, replacing the wood in the bat with nothing at all would make for an even lighter bat and, thus, provide more of an advantage. The problem here is that an empty core would increase the likelihood that the bat would break; at the very least, it would cause a suspicious, hollow sound upon contact with the ball. The cork fills in the hollow area, and does so in a lightweight way.

Not everyone believes that a corked bat provides an advantage; some tests have indicated that the decreased bat density actually diminishes the force applied to the ball. But Dr. Robert Watts, a mechanical engineer at Tulane University who studies sports science, sees things differently. He concluded that corking a bat increases its speed by about 2.5 percent; consequently, the ball might travel an extra 15 to 20 feet, a distance that would add numerous home runs to a player's total over the course of his career.

In any case, we haven't heard much lately about corked bats. That's because the headlines have been dominated by players who have used steroids to cork themselves.

# THE SKINNY ON SUMO WRESTLING

Contrary to what you may believe, you don't have to be enormous to be a sumo wrestler. In some instances, being (relatively) thin works just fine.

## SUPERSIZE THEM

Historically, sumo wrestlers (*rikishis*) have been known to dent the scales from roughly 220 pounds, which would comprise the sport's version of a 98-pound weakling, to 518 pounds. But in the world of professional sumo—with its incessant hand-slapping, salt-tossing, foot-stomping, bull-rushing, and chest-bashing—bigger isn't universally or undeniably better.

In the traditional ranks of Japanese sumo, where kudos to Shinto deities to ensure healthy harvests once played as large a role as blubber-to-blubber combat, the highest order of achievers are given the honorable title *yokozuna*. (No, *yokozuna* does not translate to "Is there any more cake?")

## THE ROAD TO YOKOZUNA

To become a *yokozuna*, a wrestler must simultaneously satisfy both subjective and objective criteria. He must dominate in the *dohyo*, or ring, where two consecutive Grand Tournament wins are considered a nifty way to attract the eye of Japan Sumo Association judges. He also must demonstrate a combination of skill, power, dignity, and grace. Fewer than 70 men in the centuries-old sport of sumo have ascended to this lofty tier, and most have been larger-than-life figures—literally.

The 27th *yokozuna*, known as Tochigiyama, was an exception. A star of the sport between 1918 and 1925, Tochigiyama was a comparative beanpole, at about 230 pounds. Yet he proved to be a crafty tactician, frequently moving mountains...of flesh. His won-loss record was 115–8.

At the opposite end of the spectrum loomed the mighty Musashimaru, the 67th *yokozuna*. He dominated the

18-square-foot *dohyo* while clad in his *mawashi* (not a diaper, though it looks like one) between 1999 and 2003. Musashimaru won about 75 percent of his 300 or so bouts, due in great measure to the fearsome nature of his physique. He tipped the scales at about 520 pounds, give or take a sack of bacon cheeseburgers.

Somewhere in the middle, we find perhaps the greatest of them all: Taiho, who reigned in the 1960s and became the 48th *yokozuna*. Taiho chalked up 32 tournament wins and weighed 337 pounds.

Bottom line? It isn't necessary to be a giant in order to make the grade as a sumo wrestler.

## Why Is a Marathon 26.2 Miles?

To most of us, running a marathon is incomprehensible. Driving 26.2 miles is perhaps a possibility, though only if we stop at least once for Combos. Equally incomprehensible is the number itself, 26.2. Why isn't a marathon 26.4 miles? Or 25.9? Why, oh why, is the magic number 26.2?

To answer this curious question, we must examine the history of the marathon. Our current marathon is descended from a legend about the most famous runner in ancient Greece, a soldier named Philippides (his name was later corrupted in text to Pheidippides). For much of the 5th century B.C., the Greeks were at odds with the neighboring Persian Empire; in 490 B.C., the mighty Persians, led by Darius I, attacked the Greeks at the city of Marathon. Despite being badly outnumbered, the Greeks managed to fend off the Persian troops (and ended Darius's attempts at conquering Greece).

After the victory, the legend holds, Philippides ran in full armor from Marathon to Athens—about 25 miles—to announce the good news. After several hours of running through the rugged Greek countryside, he arrived at the gates of Athens crying, "Rejoice, we conquer!" as Athenians rejoiced. Philippides then fell over dead. Despite a great deal of debate about the accuracy of this story, the legend still held such sway in the Greek popular mind that when the modern Olympic Games were revived in Athens in 1896, a long-distance running event known as a "marathon" was instituted.

How did the official marathon distance get to be 26.2 miles if the journey of Philippides was about 25? In the first two Olympic Games, the "Philippides distance" was indeed used. But things changed in 1908, when the Olympic Games were held in London. The British Olympic committee determined that the marathon route would start at Windsor Castle and end in front of the royal box in front of London's newly built Olympic Stadium, a distance that happened to measure 26 miles, 385 yards.

There was no good reason for the whims of British lords to become the standard, but 26.2 somehow got ingrained in the sporting psyche. By the 1924 Olympics in Paris, this arbitrary distance had become the standard for all marathons.

Today, winning a marathon—heck, even completing one—is considered a premier athletic accomplishment. In cities such as Boston, New York, and Chicago, thousands of professionals and amateurs turn out to participate. Of course, wiser people remember what happened to Philippides when he foolishly tried to run such a long distance. Pass the Combos.

# TUMULTUOUS BOWL GAMES

Since the first college "bowl" game was played in 1902—fittingly enough, at the Rose Bowl in California—almost every conceivable mishap, happenstance, and circumstance has occurred. Consider this trifecta of turmoil involving a player, a coach, and, in keeping with the spirit of the endeavor, a mascot.

**Wrong-Way Riegels—Rose Bowl, 1929:** Perhaps the most infamous play to ever take place during a bowl game occurred during the Rose Bowl tilt between Georgia Tech and the University of California. Midway through the second quarter, Golden Bear center Roy Riegels recovered a Georgia fumble and immediately tore down the sidelines toward the end zone. There was only one problem: In his confusion after snagging the loose pigskin, Riegels ran the wrong way! The end zone he was about to reach was his own. Teammate Benny Lom, the bounciest Bear of the bunch, ran his errant buddy down, caught Wrong-Way, and tackled him on the three-yard line. Things deteriorated from bad to very bad after that. After failing to advance the ball from the shadow of the uprights, California tried to punt the pill from their own end zone. A surging Georgia scrum blocked the kick and recovered the ball for a two-point safety, which proved to be the margin of victory in Tech's 8–7 win.

**Hothead Hayes—Gator Bowl, 1978:** One of the most celebrated college coaches of all time, Woody Hayes led his Ohio State charges to 16 championships, including 13 Big Ten crowns in the 28 seasons he spent strolling the sidelines for the Buckeyes. Revered for his innovative teaching techniques, Hayes was equally renowned for his volatile temper, and it was a tantrum that eventually ended his tenure in Columbus. In the closing minutes of the 1978 Gator Bowl, the Buckeyes were trailing Clemson by a slim 17–15 margin. A last-ditch Ohio State drive was nullified when Clemson's Charlie Bauman intercepted a pass near the Buckeye bench. Bauman was forced out of bounds and into a melee of Ohio State personnel. Hayes wandered into the throng and sucker-punched Bauman in the throat, instigating a free-for-all that tarnished the reputation of both the school and its coach. The following day Hayes was dismissed by the university, bringing to an inglorious end one of the game's most illustrious careers.

**Prancing Ponies—Orange Bowl, 1985:** Since 1964, tradition at Oklahoma has been that every home-field score by the Sooners is commemorated with a victory lap by the Sooner Schooner, a covered wagon pulled by a pair of Shetland ponies dubbed Boomer and Sooner. However, in the 1985 Orange Bowl, it was a case of "too soon to Schooner" that proved to be the downfall of Oklahoma's bid to wipe out the University of Washington and win the Orange Bowl. With the score tied at 14–14, the Sooners drove down the field and kicked a field goal that appeared to give them a three-point cushion. In customary fashion, it was wagons-ho as Boomer and Sooner rumbled onto the field to signify the score. Unfortunately, the ponies' prance was premature, because a penalty had been called, thereby nullifying the play. Adding insult to error, the wagon's wheels became stuck in the soggy turf, and another penalty was flagged against the Oklahoma team. The Sooners missed the ensuing field goal attempt and played the remainder of the match in a lackluster slumber, eventually losing what would become known as the Sooner Schooner Game by a score of 28–17.

## LIMIT: ONE BOWL, PLEASE
- Aluminum Bowl—Little Rock, Arkansas (1956)
- Aviation Bowl—Dayton, Ohio (1961)
- Bluegrass Bowl—Louisville, Kentucky (1958)
- Boys Bowl—Houston, Texas (1946)
- Cement Bowl—Allentown, Pennsylvania (1962)
- Glass Bowl—Toledo, Ohio (1946)

# UNUSUAL COLLEGE MASCOTS

**Aggies (Texas A&M, New Mexico State, Utah State, and others):** It's worth remembering that many land-grant schools early on taught mainly agriculture, so their students—and sometimes their teams—were called Farmers. "Aggies" grew as slang for this, and many of these schools now embrace the name proudly.

**Banana Slugs (University of California–Santa Cruz):** If a slug suggests a lethargic or reluctant team, that's just what students had in mind when they chose the image. The bright yellow banana slug lives amid the redwoods on campus and represents a mild protest of the highly competitive nature of most college sports.

**Boll Weevils/Cotton Blossoms (University of Arkansas–Monticello, men/women):** When cotton ruled Dixie, the boll weevil was more fearsome than any snake. Evidently, the women's teams didn't care to be named after an invasive insect, and who can blame them?

**Cardinal (Stanford):** It's the color, not the bird. That sounds odd until you consider the Harvard Crimson, Dartmouth Big Green, Syracuse Orange, etc. The university's overall symbol, however, is a redwood tree. A person actually dresses up as a redwood mascot, but the effect is more like a wilting Christmas tree than a regal conifer.

**Crimson Tide (University of Alabama):** The school's teams have always worn crimson, but the term "Crimson Tide" seems to have been popularized by sportswriters waxing poetic about epic struggles in mud and rain.

**Eutectics (St. Louis College of Pharmacy, Missouri):** "Eutectic" refers to the chemical process in which two solids become a liquid, representing the school's integration of competitive athletics and rigorous academic programs. ESPN recognized the Eutectic—a furry creature dressed in a lab coat—as one of the most esoteric mascots in the country.

**Governors (Austin Peay, Tennessee):** This one made sense, as the school is named for the Tennessee governor who signed the bill establishing it. At least "Governors" is more inspiring than the old nickname, "Normalities." One wonders how the eminent statesman would react to the popular student cheer today: "Let's go Peay!"

**Ichabods (Washburn University, Kansas, men):** An Ichabod would be, at the least, a generous man. The university was established as Lincoln College, but it ran out of money. When philanthropist Ichabod Washburn bailed out Lincoln, the grateful school renamed itself. This may disappoint everyone who references the headless ghost in *The Legend of Sleepy Hollow*, but Washburn University's version is still a worthy tale. The women's teams are the Lady Blues.

**Jennies (Central Missouri State, women):** A jenny is a female donkey, but this name makes sense only when put in context: The school's men's teams are the Mules. Both are a big improvement on "Normals" and "Teachers," the names used before 1922.

**Nanooks (University of Alaska–Fairbanks):** Nanuq is Inupiaq (northern Arctic Eskimo) for a polar bear. Many UAF students insist that it refers to a character in the 1922 silent ethnography film *Nanook of the North*, but to avoid controversy, perhaps, the school administration sticks firmly to the nanuq story.

**Paladins (Furman University, South Carolina):** A paladin is a pious, righteous knight. The title originally belonged to the 12 peers of Charlemagne's court.

**Poets (Whittier College, California):** If opponents don't exactly tremble when the Whittier mascot takes the field, it's because he's a bigheaded figure who dresses in colonial garb and carries a pen and pad. The school was named for poet John Greenleaf Whittier.

**Ragin' Cajuns (University of Louisiana–Lafayette):** The name refers, of course, to the region's feisty Cajun ethnic heritage. Fans hold up signs saying "Geaux Cajuns!" Although decidedly not French, it certainly gets the message across.

**Rainbow Wahine (University of Hawaii, women):** Hawaii has an interesting situation because it chose to let its teams name themselves by sport. Some men's teams are the Warriors, some are the Rainbows, and some are the Rainbow Warriors. The women have been more consistent, all using Rainbow Wahine (wahine is Hawaiian for "women").

**Stormy Petrels (Oglethorpe University, Georgia):** The name refers to a plucky shore bird that dives straight into heavy surf to find its food.

**Tarheels (University of North Carolina):** There's a lot of history at UNC, the nation's first state university. A Tarheel is a North Carolinian, though some use it to refer to rural folk in general. The legend says that North Carolinian soldiers in Civil War Confederate service remained "stuck" to the ground as if they had tar on their heels. Inexplicably, the school uses a live ram as its mascot.

**Toreros (University of San Diego, California):** Since 1961, USD teams have gone by this Spanish name for bullfighters. Unlike "matador" (a person in a fancy suit with rapier and cape), torero refers to all members of a bullfighting squad—making it an appropriate team name.

**Warhawks (University of Louisiana–Monroe):** One of college sports' newest mascots, the Warhawk represents the World War II fighter plane used by Louisianan Claire Chennault's American Volunteer Group in China, better known as the Flying Tigers. The logo, however, depicts a bird rather than a monoplane fighter.

# THE DIRT ON DRIBBLING

There are numerous rules on how to properly dribble a basketball, but bouncing the ball with such force that it bounds over the head of the ball handler is not illegal.

Although it might fun-up the standard NBA game to see players drumming dribbles with the exaggerated effort of the Harlem Globetrotters, it wouldn't do much to move the game along. And contrary to popular belief, there is no restriction on how high a player may bounce the ball, provided the ball does not come to rest in the player's hand.

Anyone who has dribbled a basketball can attest to the fact it takes a heave of some heft to give the globe enough momentum to lift itself even to eye-level height. Yet, the myth about dribbling does have some connection to reality. When Dr. James Naismith first drafted the rules for the game that eventually became known as basketball, the dribble wasn't an accepted method of moving the ball. In the game's infancy, the ball was advanced from teammate to teammate through passing. When a player was trapped by a defender, it was common practice for the ball carrier to slap the sphere over the head of his rival, cut around the befuddled opponent, reacquire possession of the ball, and then pass it up court. This innovation was known as the overhead dribble, and it was an accepted way to maneuver the ball until the early part of the 20th century. The art of "putting the ball on the floor" and bouncing it was used first as a defensive weapon to evade opposing players.

By the way, there is absolutely no credence to wry comments made by courtside pundits that the "above the head" rule was introduced because every dribble that former NBA point guard Muggsy Bogues took seemed to bounce beyond the upper reaches of his diminutive 5'3" frame.

# What's the Slowest-Moving Object In the World?

Jet cars and supersonic airplanes get all the glory for their high-speed records, but there are some objects that are just as notable for their amazing slowness. In fact, they move so slowly that scientists need special equipment to detect their movement. What moves slowest of all? The answer just might be right under your feet.

The surface of the earth is covered by tectonic plates, rigid slabs made of the planet's crust and the brittle uppermost mantle below, called the lithosphere. Some of the plates are enormous, and each is in constant movement—shifting, sliding, or colliding with other plates or sliding underneath to be drawn back down into the deep mantle. The plates "float" on the lower mantle, or asthenosphere; however, the lower mantle is not a liquid, but it is subjected to heat and pressure, which softens it so that it can flow very, very slowly.

When an earthquake occurs, parts of the plates can move very suddenly. Following the Great Alaska Earthquake in 1964, America's largest ever, the two plates involved shifted about 30 feet by the end of the event. However, most of the time tectonic plates move relatively steadily and very slowly. Scientists use a technique called Satellite Laser Ranging (SLR) to detect their movement.

SLR relies on a group of stations spread around the world that use lasers to send extremely short pulses of light to satellites equipped with special reflective surfaces. The time it takes for the light to make the round-trip from the satellite's main reflector is instantaneously measured. According to the U.S. Geological Survey, this collection of measurements "provides instantaneous range measurements of millimeter level precision" that can be used in numerous scientific applications. One of those applications is measuring the movement of Earth's tectonic plates over time.

How slow do tectonic plates move? The exact speed varies: The slowest plates move at about the same rate of speed that your fingernails grow, and the fastest plates move at about the same rate that your hair grows. A rough range is one to 13 centimeters per year. The fastest plates are the oceanic plates, and the slowest are the continental plates. At the moment the Slowest Object Award is a tie between the Indian and Arabian plates, which are moving only three millimeters per year.

If you're wondering who the runner-up is in the race to be slowest, it appears to be glaciers. The slowest glaciers creep a few inches each day, still faster than tectonic plates. However, some glaciers are so speedy they can cover nearly eight miles in a single year, and sometimes a glacier can surge. In 1936, the Black Rapid's Glacier in Alaska galloped toward a nearby lodge and highway, averaging 53 meters a day over three months. That leaves tectonic plates in the dust.

# Why Is the Sky Blue?

What if the sky were some other color? Would a verdant
green inspire the same placid happiness that a brilliant
blue sky does? Would a pink sky be tedious for everyone
except girls under the age of 15? What would poets and
songwriters make of a sky that was an un-rhymable orange?

We'll never have to answer these questions, thanks to a
serendipitous combination of factors: the nature of sunlight,
the makeup of Earth's atmosphere, and the sensitivity of
our eyes.

If you have seen sunlight pass through a prism, you know
that light, which to the naked eye appears to be white, is
actually made up of a rainbow-like spectrum of colors: red,
orange, yellow, green, blue, and violet. Light energy travels
in waves, and each of these colors has its own wavelength.
The red end of the spectrum has the longest wavelength,
and the violet end has the shortest.

The waves are scattered when they hit particles, and the
size of the particles determines which waves get scattered
most effectively. As it happens, the particles that make
up the nitrogen and oxygen in the atmosphere scatter
shorter wavelengths of light much more effectively than
longer wavelengths. The violets and the blues in sunlight
are scattered most prominently, and reds and oranges are
scattered less prominently.

However, since violet waves are shorter than blue waves, it would seem that violet light would be more prolifically scattered by the atmosphere. So why isn't the sky violet? Because there are variations among colors that make up the spectrum of sunlight—there isn't as much violet as there is blue. And because our eyes are more sensitive to blue light than to violet light, blue is easier for our eyes to detect. That's why, to us, the sky is blue.

## FAST FACTS ABOUT SPACE

- Skylab, the first American space station, fell to Earth in thousands of pieces in 1979. Thankfully, most of them landed in the ocean.

- Skylab astronauts grew one-and-a-half to two-and-a-quarter inches due to spinal lengthening and straightening as a result of zero gravity.

- The cosmos contains approximately 50 billion galaxies.

- Since 1959, more than 6,000 pieces of "space junk" (abandoned rocket and satellite parts) have fallen out of orbit, and many of these have hit Earth's surface.

- The surface gravity of Jupiter is more than two-and-a-half times greater than that of Earth.

- Uranus is unique among the planets in that its equatorial plane is almost perpendicular to the orbital plane.

- If you could fly across our galaxy from one side to the other at light speed, it would take 100,000 years to make the trip.

- Every year the sun loses 360 million tons.

- If you attempted to count the stars in a galaxy at a rate of one every second, it would take about 3,000 years to complete the task.

- Earth is the only planet in our solar system not named after a god.

- Neptune takes 165 Earth years to get around the sun. It appears blue because it is made of methane gas. Winds on Neptune can reach 1,200 miles per hour. Neptune has eight moons.

- Objects weigh slightly less at the equator than at the poles.

- According to scientists, gold exists on Mars, Mercury, and Venus.

# Why Do Space Shuttle Astronauts Wear Parachutes?

It seems like parachutes wouldn't do much good, but they're part of an escape system devised by NASA for Space Shuttle missions after the 1986 *Challenger* disaster, in which seven astronauts died when a rocket booster exploded shortly after liftoff.

## BAILING OUT

The parachutes that astronauts now wear are part of a coordinated plan that offers them a chance to bail out if problems arise during launch or landing. For obvious reasons, jumping from the shuttle is impossible while its rockets are firing. But there are scenarios in which escape would be an option. One would be after the rockets finish firing but before the shuttle reaches space. Another would be if the rockets fail after launch and the astronauts face a dangerous emergency landing in the ocean.

How would an escape work? First, the crew would guide the shuttle to an altitude of about 25,000 to 30,000 feet—just lower than the altitude reached by commercial airline flights—and jump from the shuttle through a side hatch.

To avoid hitting a wing or an engine pod during their escape, the astronauts would extend a 12-foot pole from the side of the shuttle, hook themselves to it, slide down, and jump from there. NASA's space suits are designed to work automatically during an escape. The parachute opens at 14,000 feet, and when the suit detects impact with water, the parachute detaches.

## MORE LIFE-SAVING GADGETS

The astronauts have other gizmos up their sleeves (and pant legs) that help in an emergency. When water is detected, the suit automatically deploys a life preserver. Also contained within the suit is a life raft, complete with a bailing cup to remove water that sloshes into it. Once safely afloat, the astronaut can pull a set of flares from one leg pocket and an emergency radio from the other. The suit, which is designed to keep the astronaut alive for 24 hours, is pressurized, thermal, and even comes equipped with a supply of drinking water.

The explosion that killed the *Challenger* crew was sudden and caused instant death, so this escape system would not have helped them. But because of that tragedy, today's Space Shuttle astronauts are better prepared if they need to make a daring escape.

# LAIKA THE SPACE DOG

The first occupied spacecraft did not carry a human being or even a monkey. Instead, scientists launched man's best friend.

The Space Age officially began on October 4, 1957, when the Soviet Union launched humanity's first artificial satellite, *Sputnik I*. The world sat stunned, and the space race experienced its first victory. Even more astounding was the launch of *Sputnik II* on November 3. *Sputnik II* carried the first living creature into orbit, a mongrel dog from the streets of Moscow named Laika.

## A 20TH-CENTURY DOG

A three-year-old stray that weighed just 13 pounds, Laika had a calm disposition and slight stature that made her a perfect fit for the cramped capsule of *Sputnik II*. In the weeks leading up to the launch, Laika was confined to increasingly smaller cages and fed a diet of a special nutritional gel to prepare her for the journey.

*Sputnik II* was a 250-pound satellite with a simple cabin, a crude life-support system, and instruments to measure Laika's vital signs. After the success of the *Sputnik I* launch, Soviet Premier Nikita Khrushchev urged scientists to launch another satellite on November 7, 1957, to mark the anniversary of the Bolshevik Revolution. Although work was in progress for the more sophisticated satellite eventually known as *Sputnik III*, it couldn't be completed in time. Sergei Korolev, head of the Soviet space program, ordered his team to design and construct *Sputnik II*. They had less than four weeks.

## THE FIRST CREATURE IN SPACE

The November launch astonished the world. When the Soviets announced that Laika would not survive her historic journey, the mission also ignited a debate in the West regarding the treatment of animals. Initial reports suggested that Laika survived a week in orbit, but it was revealed many years later that she only survived for roughly the first five hours. The hastily built craft's life-support system failed, and Laika perished from excess heat. Despite her tragic end, the heroic little dog paved the way for occupied spaceflight.

# ANIMALS IN SPACE

- Between 1957 and 1966, the Soviets successfully sent 13 more dogs into space—and recovered most of them unharmed.

- Dogs were initially favored for spaceflight over other animals because scientists believed they could best handle confinement in small spaces.

- In 1959, the United States successfully launched two monkeys into space. Named Able and Baker, the monkeys were the first of their species to survive spaceflight.

# What's the Difference Between a Star and a Planet?

Even astronomers quibble over this one. In the most general terms, stars and planets can be differentiated by two characteristics: what they're made of and whether they produce their own light. According to the Space Telescope Science Institute, a star is "a huge ball of gas held together by gravity." At its core, this huge ball of gas is super-hot. It's so hot that a star produces enough energy to twinkle and glow from light-years away. You know, "like a diamond in the sky."

In case you didn't know, our own sun is a star. The light and energy it produces are enough to sustain life on Earth. But compared to other stars, the sun is only average in terms of temperature and size. Talk about star power! It's no wonder that crazed teenage girls and planets revolve around stars. In fact, the word "planet" is derived from the Greek *plan te* ("wanderer"). By definition, planets are objects that orbit around stars. As for composition, planets are made up mostly of rock (Earth, Mercury, Venus, and Mars) or gas (Jupiter, Saturn, Neptune, and Uranus).

Now hold your horoscopes! If planets can be gaseous, then just what makes Uranus different from the stars that form Ursa Major? Well, unlike stars, planets are built around solid cores. They're cooler in temperature, and some are even home to water and ice. Remember what the planet Krypton looked like in the *Superman* movies? All right, so glacial Krypton is not a real planet, but you get the point: Gaseous planets aren't hot enough to produce their own light. They may appear to be shining, but they're actually only reflecting the light of their suns.

So back to the astronomers: Just what are they quibbling about? Well, it's tough agreeing on exact definitions for stars and planets when there are a few celestial objects that fall somewhere in between the two. Case in point: brown dwarfs.

Brown dwarfs are too small and cool to produce their own light, so they can't be considered stars. Yet they seem to form in the same way stars do, and since they have gaseous cores, they can't be considered planets either. So what to call brown dwarfs? Some say "failed stars," "substars," or even "planetars." In our vast universe, there seems to be plenty of room for ambiguity.

# YOU SAY URANUS, I SAY GEORGE

Its name has been the butt of countless bad jokes, but was the planet Uranus—the dimmest bulb in our solar system and nothing more than a celestial conglomeration of hydrogen, helium, and ice—first known as George?

There's actually more truth than rumor in this story, but the lines of historical fact and fiction are blurred just enough to make the discovery and naming of the seventh planet fascinating. The heavenly globe that eventually was saddled with the name Uranus had been seen for years before it was given its just rewards. For decades, it was thought to be simply another star and was even cataloged as such under the name 34 Tauri (it was initially detected in the constellation Taurus). Astronomer William Herschel first determined that the circulating specimen was actually a planet. On the evening of March 13, 1791, while scanning the sky for the odd and unusual, Herschel spotted what he first assumed was a comet.

After months of scrutiny, Herschel announced his discovery to a higher power, in this case the Royal Society of London for the Improvement of Natural Knowledge, which agreed that the scientist had indeed plucked a planet out of the night sky. King George III was duly impressed and rewarded Herschel with a tidy bursary to continue his research. To honor his monarch, Herschel named his discovery Georgium Sidus, or George's Star, referred to simply as

George. This caused some consternation among Herschel's contemporaries, who felt the planet should be given a more appropriate—and scientific—appellation. It was therefore decided to name the new planet for Uranus, the Greek god of the sky. Let the mispronunciations begin!

# BEWARE OF KILLER PLANTS

There are some obvious ways you could be killed by a plant: A tree could fall on you or twist your car into a pretzel if you veer off the road. But the more gruesome scenarios involve eating something you shouldn't. Here's a sampling from the menu of killer plants:

• Aconitum (aconite, monkshood, or wolfsbane) will start your mouth burning from the first nibble. Then you'll start vomiting, your lungs and heart will shut down, and you'll die of asphyxiation. As luck would have it, your mind will stay alert the entire time. And you don't even have to eat aconitum to enjoy its effects: Just brush up against it and the sap can get through your skin.

• Hemlock is another particularly nasty snack. In fact, the ancient Greeks gave it to prisoners who were condemned to die (including Socrates). Ingest some hemlock and it will eventually paralyze your nervous system, causing you to die from lack of oxygen to the brain and heart. Fortunately, if you happen to have an artificial ventilation system nearby, you can hook yourself up and wait about three days for the effects to wear off. But even if there is a ventilation system handy, it's best if you just don't eat hemlock.

• Oleander is chock full of poisony goodness, too. Every

part of these lovely ornamental plants is deadly if ingested. Just one leaf can be fatal to a small child, while adults might get to enjoy up to ten leaves before venturing into the big sleep. Even its fumes are toxic—never use Oleander branches as firewood. Oleander poisoning will affect most parts of your body: the central nervous system, the skin, the heart, and the brain. After the seizures and the tremors, you may welcome the sweet relief of the coma that might come next. Unfortunately, that can be followed by death.

So, while there is no need to worry about any plants sneaking up on you from behind with a baseball bat, there are plenty of reasons not to take a nibble out of every plant you see.

# Are the Colors of the Rainbow Always In the Same Order?

Yes. The order of the colors—red, orange, yellow, green, blue, indigo, and violet—from the top of the rainbow to the bottom, never changes. You may see a rainbow missing a color or two at its borders, but the visible colors always will be in the same order.

Rainbows are caused by the refraction of white light through a prism. In nature, water droplets in the air act as prisms. When light enters a prism, it is bent ever so slightly. The different wavelengths of light bend at different angles, so when white light hits a prism, it fans out. When the wavelengths are separated, the visible wavelengths appear as a rainbow.

The colors of a rainbow always appear in the same order because the wavelengths of the visible color spectrum always bend in the same way. They are ordered by the length of their waves. Red has the longest wavelength, about 650 nanometers. Violet has the shortest, about 400 nanometers. Orange, yellow, blue, and indigo have wavelengths that fall between red and violet.

The human eye is incapable of seeing light that falls outside these wavelengths. Light with a wavelength shorter than 400 nanometers is invisible; we refer to it as ultraviolet light. Likewise, light with a wavelength longer than 650 nanometers cannot be seen; we call it infrared light.

Now, about that pot of gold at the end of a rainbow—how do you get to it? If we knew that, we'd have better things to do than answer these silly questions.

# Do Rivers Always Flow North to South?

No, rivers are not subject to any natural laws that compel them to flow north to south. Only one thing governs the direction of a river's flow: gravity.

Quite simply, every river travels from points of higher elevation to points of lower elevation. Most rivers originate in mountains, hills, or other highlands. From there, it's always a long and winding journey to sea level.

Many prominent rivers flow from north to south, which perhaps creates the misconception that all waterways do so. The Mississippi River and its tributaries flow in a southerly direction as they make their way to the Gulf of Mexico. The Colorado River runs south toward the Gulf of California, and the Rio Grande follows a mostly southerly path.

But there are many major rivers that do not flow north to south. The Amazon flows northeast, and both the Nile and the Rhine head north. The Congo River flaunts convention entirely by flowing almost due north, then cutting a wide corner and going south toward the Atlantic Ocean.

There's a tendency to think of north and south as up and down. This comes from the mapmaking convention of sketching the world with the North Pole at the top of the illustration and the South Pole at the bottom.

But rivers don't follow the conventions of mapmakers. They're downhill racers that will go anywhere gravity takes them.

# WEIRD WEATHER

We've all heard that neither rain, snow, sleet nor hail, will stop our determined mail carriers, but how about a few rounds of ball lightning or tiny frogs dropping from the sky? Apparently, Mother Nature has a sense of humor. Here are some of the weirdest weather phenomena encountered on planet Earth.

## GOODNESS, GRACIOUS, GREAT BALLS OF LIGHTNING!

Perhaps it was ball lightning, an unexplained spherical mass of electrical energy, that Jerry Lee Lewis was singing about in the popular tune "Great Balls of Fire." In 1976, the strange phenomenon supposedly attacked a woman in the UK as she ironed during an electrical storm. A ball of lightning emerged from her iron, spun around the room, and then threw her across the room, ripping off half her clothes in the process. In 1962, a Long Island couple was astounded to see a fiery, basketball-size orb roll into their living room through an open window. The fireball passed between the pair, continued through the room, and disappeared down an adjacent hallway. Exactly how lightning or any other electrical anomaly can form itself into a ball and zigzag at different speeds is not well understood.

## OTHERWORLDLY LIGHTS: ST. ELMO'S FIRE

A weird haze of light glimmering around a church steeple during a storm, a rosy halo over someone's head, or a ghostly light swirling around the mast of a wave-tossed ship—these are all possible manifestations of the strange, bluish-white light known as St. Elmo's Fire, which may be a signal that a lightning strike to the glowing area is imminent. The light is a visible, electric discharge produced by heavy storms. It was named after St. Erasmus, aka St. Elmo, the patron saint of sailors.

## WHEN THE MOON GETS THE BLUES

Everyone understands that the phrase "once in a blue moon" refers to a very unusual occurrence, since blue moons are rare. But a blue moon is not actually blue. In fact, a blue moon is determined by the calendar, not by its color.

Typically, there is one full moon per month, but occasionally, a second full moon will sneak into a monthly cycle. When this happens, the second full moon is referred to as a "blue moon," which happens every two to three years. But at times, the moon has been known to appear blue, or even green, often after a volcanic eruption leaves tiny ash and dust particles in Earth's atmosphere.

## GREEN FLASH: WHEN THE SUN GOES GREEN

The term *green flash* may sound like a comic book superhero, but it is actually a strange flash of green light that appears just before the sun sinks into the horizon. Some have suggested that rare fluctuations in solar winds may be responsible for green glows and flashes that sometimes appear in the atmosphere just before sunset. Some believe it's just a mirage. But others contend that a green flash occurs when layers of the earth's atmosphere act like a prism. Whatever causes the emerald hue, seeing a flash of green light along the horizon can be an eerie and unsettling experience.

## LAVA LAMPS IN THE SKY: AURORA BOREALIS

Like a neon sign loosened from its tubing, the aurora borealis sends multicolored arches, bands, and streams of luminous beauty throughout the northern skies whenever solar flares are at their height. This occurs when electrons ejected from the sun's surface hit Earth's atmospheric particles and charge them until they glow. The electrons are attracted to Earth's magnetic poles, which is why they are seen mainly in the far northern or southern latitudes. In the Southern Hemisphere, they are called *aurora australis*. *Aurora polaris* refers to the lights of either pole.

## IT'S RAINING FROGS!

Startling as the thought of being pelted from above by buckets of hapless amphibians may be, reports of the sky raining frogs have occurred for so long that the problem was even addressed in the first century A.D., when a Roman scholar, Pliny the Elder, theorized that frog "seeds" were already present in the soil. But in 2005, residents of Serbia were shocked when masses of teensy toads tumbled out of a dark cloud that suddenly appeared in the clear blue sky. *Scientific American* reported a frog fall over Kansas City, Missouri, in July 1873, in numbers so thick they "darkened the air." And in Birmingham, England, the froglets that reportedly dropped from the heavens on June 30, 1892, were not green but a milky white. In 1987, pink frogs fell in Gloucestershire, England. No one knows for certain why this happens, but one theory is that the small animals—fish, birds, and lizards are also common—are carried from other locations by tornadoes or waterspouts.

## SPOUTING OFF

Ancient people feared waterspouts and understandably so. Waterspouts are actually tornadoes that form over a body of water, whirling at speeds as fast as 190 miles per hour. Waterspouts start with parent clouds that pull air near the surface into a vortex at an increasing rate, until water is pulled up toward the cloud. One of the world's top waterspout hot spots is the Florida Keys, which may see as many as 500 per year. They can also occur in relatively calm areas such as Lake Tahoe, on the California–Nevada border. There, a Native American legend said that waterspouts, which they called "waterbabies," appeared at the passing of great chiefs to take them to heaven.

## MIRAGES: OPTICAL CONFUSION

Mirages have been blamed for everything from imaginary waterholes in deserts to sightings of the Loch Ness Monster. They come in two forms: hallucinations or environmental illusions based on tricks of light, shadow, and atmosphere. In April 1977, residents of Grand Haven, Michigan, were able to plainly see the shimmering lights of Milwaukee, Wisconsin, some 75 miles across Lake Michigan. The sighting was confirmed by the flashing pattern of Milwaukee's red harbor beacon. Another rare type of water mirage is the *fata morgana*, which produces a double image that makes mundane objects look gigantic and may account for some reports of sea monsters.

# How Do Astronauts Go to the Bathroom?

Weightlessness sure seems fun. You see those astronauts effortlessly floating around, mugging for the camera, and magically spinning their pens in midair. But what you don't get to see is what happens when nature calls.

## THE FINAL FRONTIER

You can be sure that as much as astronauts enjoy swimming through the air like waterless fish, there's one place on Earth where all astronauts thank their lucky stars for gravity: the bathroom.

On the Space Shuttle, the astronaut sits on a commode with a hole in it, not unlike a normal toilet—except for the restraints that fit over the feet and thighs to prevent his or her body from floating away. Suction takes the place of gravity, so the seat is cushioned, which allows the astronaut's posterior to form an airtight seal around the hole. If everything is situated properly, the solid waste goes down the main hole: A separate tube with a funnel on the end takes care of the liquids. Since there's so much going on, relaxing with a newspaper is not really an option.

Today's astronauts have it easy compared to their forebears on the Apollo missions (1961–1975). When an Apollo astronaut had to go number two, he attached a specially designed plastic bag to his rear end. The bag had an adhesive flange at its opening to ensure a proper seal.

But if you think that this procedure couldn't have been any more undignified, consider this: There was no privacy. The astronauts would usually carry on with their duties while they were, you know, doing their duty. In the words of Apollo astronaut Rusty Schweickart, "You just float around for a while doing things with a bag on your butt." With no gravity and no suction, getting the feces to separate from the body was, generally, an hour-long process. It began with removing the bag—very carefully—and ended with lots and lots of wiping.

## WASTE MANAGEMENT

Where does all this stuff go? Fecal material is dried, compressed, and stored until the ship returns to Earth. (Some scientists believe that manned missions to Mars will require waste to be recycled and used for food. If you were hoping to sign up for one of those flights, you may want to think twice before dropping your application in the mail.) Urine, on the other hand, is expelled into space. The memory of this procedure caused Schweickart to wax darn-near poetic, calling a urine dump at sunset, "one of the most beautiful sights" he saw in space.

"As the stuff comes out and hits the exit nozzle," Schweickart went on, "it instantly flashes into 10 million little ice crystals, which go out almost in a hemisphere. The stuff goes in every direction, all radially out from the spacecraft at relatively high velocity. It's surprising, and it's an incredible stream of...just a spray of sparklers almost. It's really a spectacular sight."

And you thought stars looked cool.

# THE REAL DIRT ON THE DESERT

Sand dunes, scorching heat, mirages. If this is your image of the desert, you're in for a surprise. There are many stories about the desert that have spawned numerous myths. Here are two favorites.

## MYTH:

It never snows in the desert.

## FACT:

Believe it or not, the largest desert on Earth is Antarctica, where it snows a lot—the mean annual precipitation ranges from 5.9 to 10.2 inches. So why is Antarctica considered a desert? The definition of a desert is a region that receives very little rain. To be precise, a desert landscape exists where rainfall is less than 10 inches per year. Rain, of course, is needed to sustain certain types of plants and animals, but snow doesn't count as rain. So Antarctica—with all its wet snow—is dry enough to be considered a desert and too dry for a person to survive without water.

## MYTH:

Most sandstorms occur in hot, dry deserts.

## FACT:

It's true that dangerous sandstorms commonly occur in hot, dry deserts, including the Sahara and the Gobi. But they also occur frequently in a place you might never consider—North China, particularly around the area of Beijing.

A 10-year research project found that sandstorms affecting China were closely related to the cold front from Siberia, according to the Inner Mongolia Autonomous Regional Meteorological Station. As the cold front swirls through the Gobi and other large desert areas, it often combines with cyclones in Mongolia, consequently bringing sandstorms to China. So if you're planning a trip to the Great Wall of China, prepare to dust yourself off!

## MURDER, INC.

A gun; an ice pick; a rope; these were some of the favorite tools of Albert Anastasia, notorious mob assassin. When he wasn't pulling the trigger himself, this head of Murder, Inc.— the enforcement arm of New York's Five Families Mafia— was giving the orders to kill, beat, extort, and rob on the mob-controlled waterfronts of Brooklyn and Manhattan.

Born in Italy in 1902 as Umberto Anastasio, Anastasia worked as a deck hand before jumping ship in New York, where he built a power base in the longshoremen's union. Murder was his tool to consolidate power. Arrested several times in the 1920s, his trials were often dismissed when witnesses would go missing. It wasn't long before he attracted the attention of mob "brain" Lucky Luciano and subsequently helped whack Joe "the Boss" Masseria in 1931, an act that opened the way for Luciano to achieve national prominence within the organization.

Luciano put Anastasia, Bugsy Siegel, and Meyer Lanksy in charge of what became known as Murder, Inc., the lethal button men of the Brooklyn Mafia. With his quick temper and brutal disposition, Anastasia earned the nickname "Lord High Executioner."

A psychopathic assassin named Abe "Kid Twist" Reles was a key man of Murder, Inc., but turned prosecution witness when he was arrested in 1940. Reles fingered Anastasia, only to mysteriously "fall" from his hotel room while under police protective custody.

## A HISTORY OF VIOLENCE

Anastasia climbed the next rung in the mob ladder by ordering the violent 1951 deaths of the Mangano brothers and ultimately taking over the Mangano family. Eventually, however, he alienated two powerful rivals, Vito Genovese and Meyer Lansky. On October 25, 1957, as Albert Anastasia dozed in a barber's chair at New York's Park Sheraton Hotel, he was riddled by two masked gunmen (possibly Larry and Joe Gallo), who acted on orders from Genovese.

Anastasia had evaded justice for decades, but he couldn't escape the violence he himself cultivated in organized crime.

# CRIMINALS BEHAVING NICELY?

The following mixture of life's flotsam proves far and away that, like books, people can't always be judged by their covers.

## JOHN DILLINGER

Seen as a modern-day Robin Hood by many cash-strapped, Depression-era citizens, bank robber Dillinger took what he wanted when he wanted it. The public, angry at banks and the government for doing little to help them, cheered for the antihero's escape, but they weren't looking at the full picture. Dillinger and his gang were responsible for at least 10 murders. And unlike Robin Hood, Dillinger didn't share his ill-gotten booty with those in need. Nevertheless, his charm carried him along until one fateful day when he agreed to meet the now-infamous "Lady in Red" (Ana Cumpanas) at

Chicago's Biograph Theater. Unbeknownst to the gangster, Miss Cumpanas had sold him out to federal agents who had come to apprehend him. In the end, the popular gangster was cut down by a hail of bullets—a fitting end for a not-so-nice criminal.

## JOHN GOTTI

It's amazing what a quick smile and a few block parties can do for one's popularity. Labeled the "Teflon Don" for his uncanny knack at evading prosecution, the Gambino family crime boss was beloved by his Queens, New York, neighbors. Each year, the cheerful don would stage an elaborate Fourth of July celebration, free of charge, solely for their benefit. When the Teflon finally wore off in 1992 and Gotti was convicted on murder and racketeering charges, no one defended him more passionately than his neighbors. But their faith was misplaced. In 2009, informant Charles Carneglia testified that Gotti had neighbor John Favara "dissolved in a barrel of acid" after the man accidentally killed Gotti's 12-year-old son in a car accident. So much for Gotti's good neighbor policy.

## THEODORE "TED" BUNDY

If a polite, good-looking law student on crutches asked for your assistance lifting heavy objects into his car, would you help him? For those obliging young women smitten by Bundy's boyish charm, such kindness equated to a death sentence. Bundy would be tried and convicted for the murder of Kimberly Leach, just one of more than 30 women he'd eventually admit to killing. Even Dade County Circuit Court Judge Edward D. Cowart appeared impressed by Bundy as he sentenced him to death. "You're a bright young man. You'd have made a good lawyer, and I would have loved to have you practice in front of me," said the judge in a fatherly tone. "But you went another way, partner." On January 24, 1989, 2,000 searing volts of electricity ensured that Bundy's "charm" could seduce no more.

## JOHN WAYNE GACY

Serial killer Gacy often donned a clown costume to amuse children at local hospitals. He was seen as a pillar of society, working closely with the Jaycees and other groups for community improvement. But Gacy had a dark side that could repel even the most hardened criminals. His modus operandi was to drug, torture, and rape young men before killing and burying them under his house. Gacy died at the Stateville Correctional Center in Illinois on May 10, 1994, when a lethal injection shut his circus down permanently.

# JACK GRAHAM AND A NEW ERA OF FORENSIC SCIENCE

This tale of greed and mass murder ushered in a new era of forensic science.

## LOVE'S LABOR LOST

Jack Graham's mother, Daisie King, knew her only son was no angel, but she must have hoped he'd change his ways: Barely into his 20s, Graham had little patience for lawful employment, and he had already been convicted of running illegal booze and check forgery. It's thought that King paid for her son's lawyer and anted up $2,500 in court-ordered restitution on the forgery convictions.

By 1953, however, it seemed that Graham was settling down. He married and had two children. His mother, a successful businesswoman, bought a house in Colorado for the young couple, built a drive-in restaurant, and installed Graham as its manager.

But the drive-in lost money. Graham blamed his mother's meddling in the management for the loss, but he later admitted he had skimmed receipts. He also confessed to vandalizing the place twice, once by smashing the front window and the second time by rigging a gas explosion to destroy equipment he'd used as security for a personal loan. A new pickup truck Graham bought himself mysteriously stalled on a railway track with predictable results. This too proved to be an attempt at insurance fraud.

## FLIGHT TO DOOM

In the fall of 1955, King wanted to see her daughter in Alaska, and she prepared for her trip there via Portland and Seattle. On November 1, Graham saw her off on United Air Flight 629. Eleven minutes after takeoff, the plane exploded in the sky. Forty-four people died, including Daisie King.

FBI fingerprint experts were soon at the crash site to help identify bodies. The painstaking task of gathering wreckage from over a three-mile trail of scraps started. By November 7, Civil Aeronautics investigators concluded sabotage was the probable cause of the disaster.

Criminal investigators joined the FBI technical teams. Families of passengers and crewmembers were interviewed while technicians reassembled the plane's midsection where the explosion likely occurred. In the course of sifting through wreckage, bomb fragments and explosives residue were identified.

## AVALANCHE OF EVIDENCE

Inevitably, investigators took an interest in Graham. Not only would he receive a substantial inheritance from his mother's estate, he had also taken out a $37,500 travel insurance policy on her. Moreover, he had a criminal record, and according to witnesses, a history of heated arguments with his mother.

Graham was first interviewed on November 10, and again over the following two days. In a search of his property on November 12, agents discovered a roll of primer cord in a shirt pocket and a copy of the travel insurance policy secreted in a small box. Circumstantial evidence contradicted his statements, including that provided by his wife, half-sister, and acquaintances.

Finally, Graham admitted he'd built a bomb and placed it in his mother's luggage. On November 14, he was arraigned on charges of sabotage. At the time the charge did not carry a death penalty, so he was brought back into court on November 17 and charged with first-degree murder.

## A CASE OF FIRSTS

Notwithstanding the confession, investigators continued to gather forensic evidence, putting together what may have been the most scientifically detailed case in U.S. history up to that date. The case had other firsts as well. It was the first case of mass murder in the United States via airplane explosion. Graham's trial, which began on April 16, 1956, also marked the first time TV cameras were permitted to air a live broadcast of a courtroom trial.

On May 5, 1956, the jury needed only 69 minutes to find

Graham guilty. On January 11, 1957, he was executed at Colorado State Penitentiary, remorseless to the end.

# If the Cops Break Down Your Door, Do They Have to Pay For It?

It's not unprecedented. But don't expect any of those polite officers to take time out to write you a check while they're barreling through your house. You're going to need to hire a lawyer.

Generally speaking, in cases that involve the police causing damage to private property, they're covered by a couple of legal precepts known as governmental tort immunity and sovereign immunity. Tort immunity exempts the government from having to pay for damages (it also allows the government to get away with a bunch of other stuff, but that's another story). Sovereign immunity lets the government decide whether you can sue the government. You can probably guess what the government usually decides.

Let's say you are allowed to sue. You need to prove that the cops were being negligent when they broke down your door. And history has shown that in cases of simple property damage, it's fairly rare for a court to find that police were negligent. Even if the cops break down your door and then realize they've made a mistake and really meant to break down your neighbor's door, that's still considered to be a reasonable execution of their duties.

What constitutes negligence? One example would be an officer who breaks down your door without a warrant and without a pressing need to get in immediately. If you're "lucky" enough to have that happen, well, you may be the winner of a government-subsidized shopping spree in the door department at Home Depot.

In recent years, some state and local governments have moved to scale back governmental tort immunity. But even in those places, the people who benefit from government settlements tend to be the people who suffered most—those who were injured or had relatives who were killed or were subject to extreme violations of their civil rights. When it comes to busted doors, the government still probably won't show you a whole lot of sympathy.

## OUTLANDISH LAWS

- Close the blinds! In Singapore, walking around in your house while nude is against the law—it's considered pornographic.

- In Arizona, it is illegal to refuse a person a glass of water. Aimed primarily at businesses, this law is meant to cut down on dehydration deaths among homeless people.

- British law mandates that if you are driving a car, you must be in the front seat.

- According to South Korean law, traffic officers must report all bribes they receive from motorists.

- In Providence, Rhode Island, you can buy toothpaste and mouthwash on a Sunday, but you can't buy a toothbrush.

- An Australian regulation makes it illegal for fax modems to pick up on the first ring.

- Cursing in French may sound elegant, but it's illegal in Montreal. Swearing in English is okay, though.

- Dressing in a hurry has its hazards in Thailand, where it's illegal to leave your house unless you're wearing underwear.

- Massachusetts takes its clam chowder seriously— people there are legally forbidden to put tomatoes in it.

- Members of the British Parliament are not allowed to enter the House of Commons in full armor. They can't die in Parliament, either.

- Farmers in France, be aware—you may not name your pig Napoleon.

- You may not use a feather duster to tickle a girl under the chin in Portland, Maine.

- Alabama strictly forbids wearing a fake moustache in church if it could cause laughter.

- Hawaii prohibits placing coins in one's ear.

# JEFFREY DAHMER: THE MILWAUKEE MONSTER

The Oxford Apartments in Milwaukee are gone. The seedy complex at 924 North 25th Street was torn down in 1992 to prevent the site from becoming a ghoulish tourist attraction. But the empty lot still attracts visitors hoping to see a remnant of Apartment 213 and "The Milwaukee Monster." The small one-bedroom apartment was home to charming serial killer Jeffrey Dahmer, his pet fish, and his collection of dismembered corpses.

## ONCE UPON A TIME

Jeffrey Dahmer was born in Milwaukee on May 21, 1960, and his family later moved to Ohio. He attended Ohio State University for one semester, and then enlisted in the army in 1979. After being discharged for chronic drunkenness, he eventually moved back to Wisconsin, where he lived with his grandmother.

According to his parents, Dahmer started off as a sweet boy but became increasingly withdrawn during adolescence. They noticed his preoccupation with death, but they dismissed it. Friends knew he liked to dissect roadkill. Once he even impaled a dog's head on a stick. Another time, when his father noticed foul smells coming from the garage, Jeffrey told his dad he was using acid to strip the flesh from animal carcasses. Later, his stepmother realized that he might have been cleaning human bones.

## THERE'S A FIRST TIME FOR EVERYTHING

Dahmer committed his first murder in June 1978, at age 18. While still living with his parents in Ohio, he picked up a young male hitchhiker. The two had sex, then Dahmer beat the man to death, dismembered his body, and buried him in the woods. Later, Dahmer exhumed the body, crushed the bones with a mallet, and scattered them throughout the woods. His next three victims were all men Dahmer met at gay bars and brought back to a hotel or to his grandmother's house, where he seduced, drugged, and strangled them before sexually assaulting their corpses and cutting them up.

## BAD MOVES
In September 1988, Dahmer's grandmother kicked him out because he and his friends were too loud and drank too much. The day after he moved into his own apartment, Dahmer was arrested for fondling, drugging, and propositioning a 13-year-old Laotian boy. He was sentenced to a year in prison but was released after 10 months. No one knew that he had already murdered four men.

After being released on probation for the assault, Dahmer moved back in with his grandmother. But as a stipulation of his early release, he had to find his own apartment. In May 1990, Dahmer moved to his now infamous home at the Oxford Apartments.

## MODUS OPERANDI
Living on his own, Dahmer stepped up his killing spree. Between May and July 1991, he killed an average of one person each week, until he had committed a total of 17 known murders. With few exceptions, the victims were poor, gay, nonwhite men. He would meet them in gay bars or bathhouses, drug them, strangle them, have sex with them, and then dismember them with an electric saw. He saved

some parts to eat, and some skulls he cleaned and kept as trophies. He even experimented with creating "zombies" by drilling holes into his victims' heads and injecting acid into their brains while they were still alive. For the most part, he was unsuccessful, as only one man survived for more than a few hours.

On May 27, 1991, a 14-year-old Laotian boy escaped Dahmer's apartment and ran into the streets, half-naked, drugged, and groggy. Neighbors called the police, who escorted the boy back to Dahmer's apartment. Sweet-spoken Dahmer convinced the police that it was merely a lover's spat and that the boy was an adult. The police left without doing a background check on Dahmer. If they had, they would have discovered that he was a convicted child molester still on probation. After the police left, the boy, who was the brother of the boy Dahmer had been imprisoned for molesting, became his latest victim. The next week, when neighbors saw reports of a missing boy who looked like Dahmer's "boyfriend," they contacted the police and FBI but were told that he was an adult and with his lover.

## THE ONE THAT GOT AWAY

Tracy Edwards was the one that got away. On July 22, police saw him running down the street with a handcuff on his wrist and stopped him for questioning. Edwards said a man was trying to kill him. He led the police back to Dahmer's apartment, where they found a human head in the refrigerator, an array of skulls in the closet, a barrel of miscellaneous body parts, a pot full of hands and penises, a box of stray bones, a freezer full of entrails, and snapshots of mutilated bodies in various stages of decay arranged in sexual poses. The police arrested Dahmer on the spot, ending his 13-year killing spree.

## CRAZY LIKE A FOX

At his trial, Dahmer's lawyer tried to convince the jury that his client was insane, emphasizing the heinousness of the crimes. Still, Dahmer was found sane and guilty of all 15 charges against him and was sentenced to 936 years in prison—15 consecutive life sentences.

## AND SO WE COME TO THE END

Dahmer was fairly infamous when he entered the Columbia Correctional Institute in Portage, Wisconsin. He was kept out of the main prison population to protect him from other inmates. Even so, on November 28, 1994, he was assigned to a work detail with two convicted killers: Jesse Anderson and Christopher Scarver. When the guards checked in on them after a while, Anderson and Dahmer were dead; Dahmer's skull had been crushed.

# What's the Point of Multiple Life Sentences?

There are good reasons for multiple life sentences. Judges hand down multiple sentences to go along with multiple criminal offenses. Multiple charges may be decided in the same trial, but they are still considered separate crimes and often yield separate punishments. Even in the case of life imprisonment, multiple sentences can end up being very important in the rare cases in which convictions are overturned on appeal.

Let's say a jury finds a man guilty of killing five people. The judge might sentence him to five life sentences to go along with the five charges. Even if any one of the convictions is overturned (or even if four of them are overturned), the murderer still has to carry out a life sentence. To walk free, he would have to be exonerated of all five murders.

Furthermore, "life" doesn't always mean an entire lifetime. Depending on the sentencing guidelines of the state, the judge may sentence a man to life imprisonment with the possibility of parole. In this instance life is the maximum length of the sentence, meaning that the defendant could conceivably go free if a parole board releases him after he's served the minimum time (30 years, for example). If, however, a defendant is convicted on multiple charges, the judge may hand down multiple life sentences with the possibility of parole—but the judge can also specify that those sentences be served consecutively rather than concurrently. This way the prisoner will not get a parole hearing until the minimum time for all the sentences put together has been served. Consider multiple life sentences as a safeguard.

## THE ROCK: ALCATRAZ

When people discuss famous prisons, you can bet your bottom dollar that "The Rock"—Alcatraz Island, or just Alcatraz for short—is nearly always mentioned.

For thousands of years, Alcatraz Island sat peacefully off the coast of California—until Spanish explorer Lieutenant Juan Manuel de Ayala sailed into San Francisco Bay in 1775. For a long time, the island's only inhabitants were pelicans, rocks, grass, and more pelicans. Ayala named it Isla de los Alcatraces, which means "Island of the Pelicans."

## A LESS PEACEFUL FUTURE

The island evolved into a military fortress, then during the Civil War, it served as a prison for enemy soldiers, insubordinate army personnel, and Confederate sympathizers, thus beginning its long and illustrious history.

A new prison complex was built on Alcatraz Island in 1912. The U.S. Army turned Alcatraz into a 600-cell military prison—the largest reinforced-concrete building in the world. But getting food, water, and supplies to the island became too expensive for the military.

## NEW TRENDS IN LOCKUPS

Before long, a new kind of criminal emerged—mobsters. The public needed a place to put these much-feared lawbreakers, and "escape-proof" Alcatraz provided the perfect solution. In 1934, the federal government took over Alcatraz from the military and redesigned it to strike fear in the heart of any public enemy. Significantly fortified buildings, combined with the jagged rocks of Alcatraz Island and the icy waters and strong currents of San Francisco Bay, made escape from Alcatraz seem virtually impossible.

James A. Johnston was hired as warden of Alcatraz. Under his administration, prisoners received only basic necessities. When extreme discipline was warranted, prisoners were placed in a "strip cell"—a dark, steel-encased room with a hole in the floor in which the inhabitant could relieve himself. Guards controlled the ability to flush. This institution took the concept of solitary confinement to a new level. The strip cell got its name because inmates were stripped naked before entry. They were also placed on severely restricted diets. The room was kept pitch-black. A mattress was allowed at night but taken away during the daytime.

## GETTING OUT

No prisoners were sentenced directly to Alcatraz. Instead, the facility was populated with the worst inmates from other prisons. It was not until prisoners got in trouble elsewhere in the penitentiary system that they were sent to the Rock. People tried to escape over the years, but they failed miserably—until June 11, 1962, when Frank Lee Morris, Allen West, and Clarence and John Anglin executed a clever escape plan. The complex plot involved escape holes made with crude drills fashioned from kitchen equipment, human decoys, and a rubber raft made from raincoats. After a bed check, three of the inmates were never seen again, having escaped through utility corridors and ventilation shafts to the beach. Allen West, however, failed to make his escape hole large enough by the scheduled time and was left behind. The trio's escape was officially deemed to be unsuccessful—there was no evidence that any of the three survived the attempt—but the television show *MythBusters* proved that escape was indeed possible with the materials they had at hand.

# DOOMED CULTS AND SOCIAL EXPERIMENTS

## THE PEOPLE'S TEMPLE

**The Leader:** Jim Jones started his People's Temple with the idea that social justice should be available to all—even the marginalized, the poor, and minorities. He established a commune outside San Francisco in 1965 with about 80 people. Jones capitalized on the rising tide of activism in the 1960s, recruiting affluent, Northern California hippies to help the working-class families who were already members of the People's Temple. The People's Temple helped the poorer members of their group navigate the confusing social welfare system. The Temple opened a church in an impoverished section of San Francisco that provided a number of social services, such as free blood pressure testing, free sickle-cell anemia testing, and free childcare for working families.

**The Turning Point:** Not all was as it appeared inside the People's Temple. A perfect storm of complaints from disaffected members, media reports that questioned the Temple's treatment of current members, and an IRS investigation led Jones to move the People's Temple to Guyana, on the northern tip of South America. In the summer and fall of 1977, the People's Temple started what was supposed to be a utopian agricultural society, which they called Jonestown.

**The Demise:** In November 1978, U.S. Representative Leo Ryan of San Francisco led a fact-finding mission in response to constituents' concerns that members of the Temple were being kept in Guyana against their will. He offered to help anyone who wanted to leave. A few members joined him, but as the congressional party was waiting on a landing strip for transportation, attackers drove out of the jungle and shot at them. Ryan and four others were killed.

Apparently worried about the closer scrutiny all this could bring, on November 18, Jones ordered his followers to commit "revolutionary suicide" by drinking Fla-Vor-Aid laced with cyanide. More than 900 members of the People's Temple died.

## THE FAMILY

**The Leader:** Charles Manson was worried about pollution and the damage it would do to the environment. Unfortunately, he manifested his concern by brainwashing teenagers and sending them on murder sprees. Manson had a hard life—spent mostly in juvenile halls, jail, and institutions. He finally ended up in San Francisco, surrounded by young women, most of whom were emotionally unstable and in love with him. With a group of these girls, he headed south to Los Angeles.

**The Turning Point:** After moving into the Spahn Ranch north of L.A., where Manson and his followers survived by scavenging food discarded from grocery stores, he started to polish what he considered his philosophy—an Armageddon in which race wars, what he called, "Helter Skelter," would break out. According to this philosophy, Manson would be the one to guide the war's aftermath and rule the world.

Reportedly in an attempt to spark these race wars, the Manson Family staged a series of mass murders, most famously those of Sharon Tate and her guests on August 9, 1969. Because of orders from Manson, four members of the Family killed Tate and her three friends. They did it, according to Susan Atkins, one of the murderers, to shock the world.

**The Demise:** Bragging to others about their murder sprees ultimately ended up undoing the Family. Friends of Manson eventually told police details of the murders. But the problem wasn't exactly finding the culprits; the problem was proving that members of the Family were responsible for the murders Manson ordered them to perform. Ultimately, a grand jury took only 20 minutes to hand down indictments in the cases against members of the Family.

## BRANCH DAVIDIANS

**The Leader:** David Koresh joined the Branch Davidians in 1981. The group had been in existence since 1955, having broken off from the Davidian Seventh-Day Adventists, which itself was a group that split with the Seventh-Day Adventist church more than 20 years before that. Koresh was amiable and flamboyant, easy-going and intelligent. After a face-off with the son of the leader of the Branch Davidians, Koresh ultimately ended up as the group's leader and spiritual guide. As all serious cult leaders know, it was important not only to establish himself as a demigod, but also to impress upon his flock the impending apocalypse and the absolute necessity of following the rules he created.

**The Turning Point:** Koresh stockpiled weapons in anticipation of inevitable attacks. He taught his followers that they should prepare for the end. He questioned their loyalty and expected them to kill themselves for the cause. On February 28, 1993, the end began. Based on reports of illegal arms sales, child abuse, and polygamy, federal agents raided the Mount Carmel Center near Waco, Texas, setting off a gunfight that ultimately set up a 51-day siege of the Branch Davidian compound.

**The Demise:** On April 19, 1993, federal agents, in an attempt to force the Davidians out, launched tear gas into the compound. Koresh and the Davidians began shooting. The agents injected more gas, and the exchange continued for several hours. About six hours after the gassing began, fires erupted inside the compound. This was followed by more gunfire in the compound, and agents on the scene reportedly believed the Davidians were either killing themselves or shooting one another. Firefighters came to the scene but were not allowed to combat the flames for some time out of fear of gunfire. After the smoke cleared, 75 people within the compound were found dead. Koresh was identified by dental records—he had been killed by a gunshot to the head.

# What's the Difference Between Mass Murders and Serial Killers?

## THE MASS MURDERER

A mass murderer kills four or more people during a short period of time, usually in one location. In most cases, the murderer has a sudden mental collapse and goes on a rampage, progressing from murder to murder without a break. About half the time, these outbreaks end in suicides or fatal standoffs with the police.

Various school shootings over the years have been instances of mass murder, as have been famous cases of postal workers "going postal." A case in which someone murders his or her entire family is a mass murder. Terrorists are lumped into this category as well, but they also make up a group of their own.

## THE SERIAL KILLER

A serial killer usually murders one person at a time (typically a stranger), with a "cooling off" period between each transgression. Unlike mass murderers, serial killers don't suddenly snap one day—they have an ongoing compulsion (usually with a sexual component) that drives them to kill, often in very specific ways.

Serial killers may even maintain jobs and normal relationships while going to great lengths to conceal their killings. They may resist the urge to kill for long periods, but the compulsion ultimately grows too strong to subjugate. After the third victim, an aspiring killer graduates from plain ol' murderer to bona fide serial killer.

## THE REST

In between these two groups, we have the spree killer and the serial spree killer. A spree killer commits murder in multiple locations over the course of a few days. This is often part of a general crime wave. For example, an escaped convict may kill multiple people, steal cars, jaywalk, and litter as he tries to escape the police. As with a mass murderer, a spree killer doesn't plan each murder individually. The serial spree killer, on the other hand, plans and commits each murder separately, serial-killer style. But he or she doesn't take time off between murders or maintain a double life. It's all killing, all the time. One of the best-known examples is the Washington, D.C.-area beltway snipers who killed 10 people within three weeks in October 2002.

Of course, if you see any of these types of killer in action, don't worry about remembering the right term when you call the police. They're all equally bad.

## INTERESTING ANIMAL LAWS

- In Alaska, you can't look at a moose from an airplane.

- In Corpus Christi, Texas, you can't raise alligators in your home.

- It's illegal to imitate an animal in Miami.

- Ohioans need a license to keep a bear.

- Utah drivers must beware: Birds have the right of way on all public highways.

- In Madison, Wisconsin, divorcing couples must be aware that joint custody is not allowed for family pets. Custody is awarded to the party who is in possession of the animal at the time of the divorce.

- In most villages, towns, and cities, it's illegal to take in a wild animal as a pet.

- In French Lick Springs, Indiana, there was once a law requiring black cats to wear bells around their necks on Friday the 13th.

- In Oregon, you can be fined up to $6,250 and face up to a year in jail if you adopt an endangered animal.

- In most jurisdictions, keeping a deer in your backyard is illegal.

- Many states, including Minnesota, Wyoming, Georgia, California, and Kentucky, ban the private ownership of primates as pets.

- In Florida, it is illegal to have sexual relations with a porcupine.

# THE NON-SUSPECTS IN POLICE LINEUPS

Appropriately enough, these "fillers" (also known as "distractors") are mostly criminals or suspected criminals. Who better to act as possible perps?

In the traditional "live" police lineup, in which a witness picks out the bad guy from behind a one-way mirror, the police typically present one actual suspect and four or five similar-looking inmates from the local jail. The lineup can be either simultaneous (with the suspect and fillers standing together) or sequential (with the possible perps coming out one by one). When there aren't enough suitable inmates, police officers and other station staff may participate. Occasionally, the police will even recruit people with the right look off the street and pay them a small fee for their trouble.

Nevertheless, it can be difficult to come up with five people who closely match the description of a suspected perpetrator. And even when such fillers can be found, the very nature of using people who bear similarities to the culprit can lead to false identifications—if one filler resembles the suspect much more closely than the other participants, he stands a pretty good chance of being identified by the witness as the perp. Furthermore, if the police choose fillers who don't closely match the description of the suspect, a judge might later rule that the lineup was unfair.

For this reason, many police departments have switched from using traditional lineups to utilizing photo arrays, also known as virtual lineups. With this method, the police select a series of mug shots that closely match the description of the suspected perpetrator. In the United States, the conventional virtual lineup includes two rows of three pictures and has been dubbed the "six pack." As with the live lineup, some police departments prefer to use a sequential virtual lineup, showing the witness only one picture at a time.

Some departments utilize software that automatically picks suitable faces from a large database of police pictures. So if you ever get arrested, be sure to smile for your mug shot—you never know who will be checking you out later.

# How Do They Salt
# Peanuts in the Shell?

No, bioengineers haven't created a super breed of naturally salty peanut plants (yet). The method isn't nearly that complicated.

To salt peanuts while they're still in the shell, food manufacturers soak them in brine (salty water). In one typical approach, the first step is to treat the peanuts with a wetting agent—a chemical compound that reduces surface tension in water, making it penetrate the shell more readily. Next, the peanuts are placed into an enclosed metal basket and immersed in an airtight pressure vessel that is filled with brine. The pressure vessel is then depressurized to drive air out of the peanut shells and suck in saltwater.

Peanuts may go through several rounds of pressurization and depressurization. Once the peanuts are suitably salty, they are rinsed with clean water and spun on a centrifuge in order to get rid of the bulk of the water. Finally, they are popped into an oven so that the drying process can be completed.

# What Exactly Is In Spam?

While your IT guy might tell you spam is an offensive unsolicited email, the original Spam was a packaged pork luncheon meat created by Jay Hormel in 1937. Nearly eight billion cans of Spam have been sold, and each year legions of fans congregate at festivals like Spamarama and Spam Jam to celebrate its meaty, salty goodness.

What is it that makes Spam, well, Spam? For starters, there's the distinctive vacuum-sealed tin. Hormel Foods Corporation says as long as no air gets into the can, Spam has a shelf life of...forever. "It's like meat with a pause button," they exult.

To that, one can only say, "Where's the remote?" After all, flavors like Hot & Spicy, Hickory Smoke, and Golden Honey Grail (a salty-sweet Spam created in honor of the Broadway musical *Monty Python's Spamalot*) are pretty hard to resist. Especially when you consider how boring regular old ham is in comparison.

Ham is from the upper part of a pig leg that's been salted and dried, or smoked. Spam, on the other hand, is a combination of ham and pork (pork being cuts from the pig shoulder or elsewhere). Add to that sugar, salt, water, a little potato starch, and a dash of sodium nitrate (for "pinkification" coloration), and you've got yourself a true meat marvel.

The history of Spam is almost as colorful as the meat itself. Spam was shipped overseas during World War II and fed to the Allied soldiers. Some over-the-top Spamheads go so far as to say the economical pork loaf helped the Allies achieve victory.

Today, Spam truly is a world power. It is made in factories all over the globe, from Austin, Minnesota, and Fremont, Nebraska, to Denmark, South Korea, and the Philippines.

As to how the luncheon meat got its name, some speculate it came from combining the words "spiced" and "ham." However, Hormel Foods says Jay Hormel held a contest to find a name. New York radio actor Kenneth Daigneau was crowned the winner, and for that he won a prize of $100.

## 15 THINGS YOU DIDN'T KNOW ABOUT POPCORN

**1.** Popcorn's scientific name is *zea mays everta*, and it is the only type of corn that will pop.

**2.** People have been enjoying popcorn for thousands of years. In 1948, popped kernels around 5,000 years old were discovered in caves in New Mexico.

**3.** It is believed that the Wampanoag Native American tribe brought popcorn to the colonists for the first Thanksgiving in Plymouth, Massachusetts.

**4.** Traditionally, Native American tribes flavored popcorn with dried herbs and spices, possibly even chili. They also made popcorn into soup and beer, and made popcorn headdresses and corsages.

**5.** Christopher Columbus allegedly introduced popcorn to the Europeans in the late 15th century.

**6.** Charles Cretors in Chicago invented the first commercial popcorn machine in 1885.

**7.** American vendors began selling popcorn at carnivals in the late 19th century. When they began to sell outside movie theaters, theater owners were initially annoyed, fearing that popcorn would distract their patrons from the movies. It took a few years for them to realize that popcorn could be a way to increase revenues. Popcorn has been served in movie theaters since 1912.

**8.** Nowadays, many movie theaters make a greater profit from popcorn than they do from ticket sales, since, for every dollar spent on popcorn, around 90 cents is pure profit. Popcorn also makes moviegoers thirsty and more likely to buy sodas.

**9.** What makes popcorn pop? Each kernel contains a small amount of moisture. As the kernel is heated, this water turns to steam. Popcorn differs from other grains in that the kernel's shell is not water-permeable, so the steam cannot escape and pressure builds up until the kernel finally explodes, turning inside out.

**10.** Unpopped kernels are called "old maids" or "spinsters."

**11.** There are two possible explanations for old maids. The first is that they didn't contain sufficient moisture to create an explosion; the second is that their outer coating (the hull) was damaged, so that steam escaped gradually, rather than with a pop. Good popcorn should produce less than 2 percent old maids.

12. Americans consume 17 billion quarts of popped popcorn each year. That's enough to fill the Empire State Building 18 times.

13. Nebraska produces more popcorn than any other state in the country—around 250 million pounds per year. That's about a quarter of all the popcorn produced annually in the United States.

14. There are at least five contenders claiming to be the "Popcorn Capital of the World" due to the importance of popcorn to their local economies, and only one of them is in Nebraska. They are: Van Buren, Indiana; Marion, Ohio; Ridgway, Illinois; Schaller, Iowa; and North Loup, Nebraska.

15. Popped popcorn comes in two basic shapes: snowflake and mushroom. Movie theaters prefer the snowflake because it's bigger. Confections such as caramel corn use the mushroom because it won't crumble.

# FALLACIES AND FACTS ABOUT FOOD

**FALLACY:** Baking soda eliminates odors in the refrigerator.

**FACT:** Chemically speaking, the alkaline composition of baking soda may absorb and neutralize a bit of an acidic odor. But the humidity in a fridge can cause the baking soda to develop a hard crust, further reducing its already weak ability to tame tough odors. Replace the baking soda with an open canister of charcoal, which will do a much better job of soaking up smells.

**FALLACY:** Lobsters scream in pain when dropped into boiling water.

**FACT:** First, lobsters have no vocal cords. Second, lobsters, crabs, and other invertebrates have ultrasimple nervous systems that lack the receptors to feel what humans call "pain." Here's the explanation for the sound you hear: Air that is trapped under the lobster's shell expands rapidly in boiling water and escapes through small openings. So in the same way that teapots don't actually whistle, lobsters don't really scream.

**FALLACY:** Thanksgiving turkey makes you sleepy.

**FACT:** Although many people believe that the culpable compound in turkey is the natural sedative known as tryptophan, plenty of other foods (including beef, pork, and cheese) contain similar or higher amounts of the amino acid. Most likely, the other things you consume at your holiday table, including the alcoholic beverages and carbohydrates that accompany Mom's turkey, can slow your metabolism. This, along with a heavy meal that forces your diaphragm to work harder (it pulls the lungs down and hinders breathing), can leave you snoring on the couch after dinner.

**FALLACY:** Raw eggs carry salmonella.

**FACT:** According to the U.S. Department of Agriculture, 1 in 3,600 eggs is contaminated with salmonella. That's 300 dozen—if your family eats a carton every week, you may get one bad egg every six years. In many cases, the contamination is on the shell rather than in the egg itself (chickens aren't the cleanest creatures in the barnyard).

The process of pasteurization, which many commercial egg plants employ, uses hot water baths to kill bacteria while keeping the egg inside the shell uncooked. When in doubt, always cook eggs completely, and be sure to purchase in-shell eggs from a dependable vendor. Also, while you're checking the carton for cracked eggs before you buy them, check the expiration date!

**FALLACY:** Food that falls on the floor is okay if picked up within five seconds.

**FACT:** Granted, the longer the contact time, the greater the amount of contamination, but food products that come into contact with any unsanitary surface can pick up pathogens in as little as two seconds. A quick retrieval may mean fewer harmful germs, but it's no assurance of safety. Bacteria can thrive on surfaces for as long as a month, so cleaning floors and countertops with a disinfectant can go a long way toward keeping your meals down—for good.

## Is There Any Duck In Duck Sauce?

If you wanted to keep things authentic, the question would be, "Are there any plums in plum sauce?" because duck sauce is a nickname that plum sauce adopted over time. However, when speaking of Chinese food, there seems to be little authenticity left.

Yong Chen, a history professor at the University of California-Irvine, says that Chinese food "is quintessentially American." Ever since the first Chinese restaurants opened in Californian mining towns in the mid-19th century, Chinese restaurateurs have looked for ways to Americanize their dishes. In China, and in better fine-dining establishments that serve Peking duck, the traditional sauce that accompanies this dish is hoisin sauce (which is soy-based), not plum sauce.

However, over time it became acceptable in the United States for plum sauce to be served with duck. Eventually—and quite logically—it took on the name duck sauce. Ed Schoenfeld, a restaurateur and Chinese food consultant, says that the Chinese condiment degraded over time as it became mass-produced.

Duck sauce is not the only Americanized fare on a Chinese restaurant menu: General Tso's chicken was once very savory, made with garlic and vinegar. Today it is a batter-fried, syrup-laden shadow of its former self. There are also a lot of items that are not at all Chinese. Chop suey and crab rangoon, as well as sweet-and-sour pork, chicken, beef, and shrimp, are all "Chinese-ified" foods. Even the fortune cookie was an idea that started in 1918 in America, though it is now popular in China. Go figure.

Just to be on the safe side, here is a list of common ingredients found in duck (plum) sauce: plums, vinegar, sugar, ginger, garlic, chiles, salt, and water. Nope, no duck.

## What's the Shelf Life of a Twinkie?

Can Hostess Twinkies really stay fresh for 50 years or more? If you were around during the Cold War in the 1950s and 1960s, when a nuclear attack from the Soviet Union seemed possible, you might believe they do.

At the height of the Cold War, Twinkies were staples of the survival foods people stocked in household bomb shelters. This helped spawn the notion that the spongy snacks could withstand not only a nuclear holocaust, but also the ravages of time.

Truth is, a Twinkie's shelf life is about 25 days. If even that seems like a lot of stay-fresh time for a baked product, consider that Twinkies are a processed, packaged food and contain no dairy ingredients that can go bad in a hurry. Like many other commercially baked goods, they're tweaked with preservatives and stabilizing trans fats.

Check the label and you'll find such ingredients as vegetable and/or animal shortening and partially hydrogenated soybean, cottonseed, or canola oil. These artificially produced fats are more solid than clear liquid oils and, thus, are less likely to spoil. They help Twinkies stay soft and tasty, though not for years or decades.

# 7 DISHES MADE FROM ENTRAILS

## 1. KOKORETSI

In Greece, it's all about lamb. Skewered, baked, roasted—if it's lamb, the Grecians are cooking it. But these folks would never waste good meat: Kokoretsi is a traditional Balkan dish often served for Easter that includes lamb intestine, heart, lung, and kidneys, or a combination of any of the above. Chunks of these organs are speared onto a skewer and then wrapped up in the small intestine, which forms a kind of sausage casing. The spear is set over a fire and sprinkled with oregano and lemon juice. In a few hours, *opah!* Grilled guts for everyone!

## 2. HAGGIS

On paper, it just doesn't look appetizing: mix sheep's heart, liver, and lung meat with oatmeal and fat, and stuff the mixture into its own stomach; boil for three hours and enjoy. Still, that's exactly what haggis is, and the Scottish have been enjoying this dish for centuries. Traditionally served in a sauce with turnips and potatoes, this dish is used also in that popular national pastime, "haggis throwing."

## 3. TRIPE

Is your stomach making those growly hungry noises? Try some stomach! Served in many countries across the globe, the stomach, known as tripe, is the main ingredient in many regional dishes. Beef tripe is the most commonly used stomach, but sheep, goat, and pig stomachs are often on the menu as well. Tripe is used often in soups and in French sausages, fried up in Filipino dishes, and used as a relish in Zimbabwe. In Ireland and Northern England, tripe is simply served up with onions and a stiff drink.

## 4. KHASH

If you're a cow, you'd better watch your step. Folks in Armenia are crazy about khash, a dish primarily made from cow's feet. First, the hooves are removed. Next, the feet are cleaned and cooked in plain boiling water overnight. By morning, the mixture is a thick broth and the meat has separated from the bone. Brain and stomach bits can be added for extra flavor. Armenians are careful about when they serve this favorite dish—it reportedly has strong healing properties—and it is usually served only on important holidays. Peppers, pickled veggies, and cheese go well with kash, but the favorite accompaniment is homemade vodka.

## 5. YAKITORI

Who doesn't like a juicy grilled chicken skewer? Look closely if you purchase one from a Japanese street vendor, however. Yakitori are chicken skewers that contain more parts of the chicken than you may care to taste, including the heart, liver, gizzard, skin, tail, small intestine, tongue, and wing.

## 6. ROCKY MOUNTAIN OYSTERS

There's not a lot on a farm animal you can't eat, as evidenced by Rocky Mountain Oysters, or bull testicles. Once the testicles of the bull (or lamb or buffalo) are removed, they're peeled, dipped in flour, and deep-fried to a golden crunch. This dish is commonly found in the American West, where bulls are prevalent, and also in bull-populated Spain.

## 7. WHITE PUDDING

To make white pudding (and if you live in Scotland, Ireland, Nova Scotia, or Iceland, you might), you'll first need a big bowl of suet, or pork fat. It's the main ingredient in this dish, which also includes meat and oatmeal, and, in some earlier recipes, sheep brains. The pudding is similar to blood pudding, but without the blood. Sometimes formed into a sausage shape, white pudding can be cooked whole, fried, or battered and served in place of fish with chips.

# Is Jell-O Made From Horses?

Could this fun, wiggly dessert be the final resting place for the likes of Black Beauty and Mister Ed? Sure. But let's not be too picky—any creature with bones can become Jell-O. It's an equal opportunity dessert.

Jell-O is made from gelatin, which is processed collagen. Collagen makes your bones strong and your skin elastic and stretchy (there's that jiggly wiggle). To make gelatin, you take bones, skin, tendons, and whatnot from animals (primarily cows or pigs), grind everything up, wash and soak it in acid (also lime, if cow parts are used), and throw it in a vat to boil. The acid or lime breaks down the components of the ground animal pieces, and the result is gelatin, among other things. The gelatin conveniently rises to the top of this mixture of acid and animal parts, creating an easy-to-remove film.

In the Victorian era, when gelatin was really catching on, it was sold in the film state. People had to clarify the gelatin by boiling it with egg whites and eggshells, which took a lot of time. In 1845, a crafty inventor patented a powdered gelatin, which was to be extracted from the bones of geese. In 1897, this powdered gelatin was named Jell-O and went on to become the line of dessert products that, to this day, we always have room for.

Why does the list of ingredients in Jell-O include gelatin and not cow and pig pieces? Because the U.S. federal government does not consider gelatin an animal product, since it is extensively processed. Gelatin is also found in gummy bears candy, cream cheese, marshmallows, and other foods.

What if you like Jell-O, cream cheese, marshmallows and such, but would rather not eat the boiled bones and skin of animals? There are alternatives. Agar and carrageenan are from seaweed and can be used to make delicious gelatinous-like goodies.

So while it's unlikely your Jell-O contains traces of Mister Ed or Black Beauty, it could test positive for Wilbur or Elsie.

# Why Are Some Chicken Eggs White and Others Brown?

This one is easy: An egg's color is determined by the breed of hen that laid it. According to the American Egg Board, breeds with white feathers and white ear lobes, such as the White Leghorn, lay white eggs. Breeds with red feathers and red ear lobes, such as the Rhode Island Red, lay brown eggs. It's that simple, but it doesn't answer other questions about white eggs and brown eggs.

For instance, have you heard that brown eggs are more nutritious than white? Whoever told you that one was 11 short of a dozen. Egg color has no effect on nutritive value or on taste, quality, or cooking performance. Once you crack the shell, white and brown eggs are the same on the inside.

It comes down to personal preference. In the United States, there is more overall demand for white eggs, so they are more commonly found in your grocer's dairy case. Take your cart for a spin at the local Stop & Shop in Greenwich,

Connecticut, however, and you may find the opposite is true. Regionally speaking, New Englanders are partial to the brown variety.

If white eggs and brown eggs are equally good, why are brown ones more expensive? The birds that lay brown eggs are slightly larger in size than their white counterparts. Consequently, they require more food to get a-laying, and that cost is passed on to consumers.

Before you go counting all your chickens, you might want to know that eggs come in more colors than just white and brown. Rare "boutique" hens, such as the Araucana, lay eggs in beautiful blue and blue-green colors. No PAAS color kit required at Easter for these eggs!

#  Why Does Bottled Water Have a "Best If Used By" Date?

In the United States, bottled water is considered a packaged food. Thus, it is regulated by the U.S. Food and Drug Administration (FDA). According to the FDA's Current Good Manufacturing Practices (CGMP), all bottled water must be sampled, analyzed, and found to be safe and sanitary. CGMP regulations specify proper bottling procedures, record keeping, and plant and equipment design.

And that's not all. Bottled water must adhere to state regulations, and bottled-water producers that are members of the International Bottled Water Association must follow that trade organization's code, which runs a stupefying 30 pages.

The different ways that bottled water can be described on the label include: spring water, purified water, mineral water, distilled water, drinking water, and artesian water. According to the FDA, carbonated water, seltzer water, soda water, sparkling water, and tonic water are soft drinks, so they are not regulated as bottled water.

What does all of this have to do with the "best if used by" date on many of the bottles of water that are consumed in the United States? Plenty. Bottled water that meets FDA requirements has an indefinite shelf life, according to the agency. Therefore, the FDA does not require bottlers to list a "best if used by" date, nor does it require an expiration date.

With bottled water, there really is no difference between an expiration date and a "best if used by" date. Major bottled-water companies such as Evian, Poland Spring, Aquafina, and Perrier, to name a few, voluntarily place expiration dates on their containers as a courtesy to customers. The water is still safe to drink after the listed date if the container has retained its seal, according to a Poland Spring spokesperson, but it could exhibit off-flavors or odors if it has not been stored properly. The typical expiration date is two years from the packaging date. Dasani, a Coca-Cola brand, stamps a one-year expiration date on its water. The popular Fiji brand uses a "best if used by" date.

The FDA Center for Food Safety and Applied Nutrition defines "best if used by" as the deadline for consuming a food to assure best flavor and quality. But if you store your bottled water unopened and in a cool place, that date might never truly arrive.

# Do Poppy Seeds Cause Positive Drug Tests?

The next time you enjoy a slice of poppy-seed cake with ice cream, you can say, "This will go straight to my hips... and perhaps straight from my urine to a positive drug test in a lab."

Depending on when you take the test, simply eating one poppy-seed bagel can lead to a positive result. Such a finding is often referred to as a "false positive." This term, however, is false in itself: The test comes back "positive" because you do have morphine in your system. But the reason you test positive is what your employer or parole officer cares about: Were you chasing the dragon or chasing the complete breakfast?

Poppy seeds contain morphine, but after being gobbled up, they don't have any drug-related effect on the body. However, the morphine is detectable in your urine, and there's no way to tell from a basic urine test whether the morphine came from heroin or a muffin.

To address this curious problem, the legal threshold for a positive drug-test result was raised in 1998. The Mandatory Guidelines for Federal Workplace Drug Testing Programs adjusted the point at which a test is considered "positive" from 300 nanograms per milliliter to 2,000 nanograms per milliliter. This revised threshold does miss a few drug abusers, but it filters out most of the positive results that are caused by the munchies. Additionally, hair testing can help to clarify which type of morphine is detected.

# Why Is Red Wine Served at Room Temperature and White Wine Chilled?

Researchers at Belgium's Katholieke Universiteit Leuven have discovered our taste buds perceive flavors differently at different temperatures. Specifically, the warmer the food or beverage in your mouth, the stronger that electric flavor signal travels from your taste receptors to your brain. That can be a good or a bad thing, depending on what you're eating or drinking. For example, frozen ice cream tastes sweeter as it melts on your tongue. But a beer tastes bitter after it's gotten warm in the sun.

But back to the grape juice. The whole point of chilling (or not chilling) a wine is to serve it at a temperature at which our taste buds will be most tantalized by it. Cold makes white wines less sweet and more refreshingly crisp and acidic. Cold helps champagnes and sparklers retain their bubbles long after you've popped the cork. As for reds, they tend to be a bit more tannic (biting) than whites, so a little warmth goes a long way in making them taste more fruity and aromatic.

Wine snobs (okay, "wine experts") will tell you that the proper serving temperature is crucial to bringing out a wine's optimum flavor, aroma, and structure (that means how it feels on your tongue). These experts will spout out general rules such as these: Sparkling wine must be served at 48 degrees Fahrenheit, white wine at 53 degrees Fahrenheit, rosé wine at 51 degrees Fahrenheit, and red wine at 62 degrees Fahrenheit.

The experts have the best intentions. After all, serving a wine too warm or too cold can negatively affect its flavor. A white that's overly frigid can taste...well, tasteless. And a red that's too toasty can seem too alcoholic, even vinegary.

What's a wine drinker without a fancy wine cellar to do? Just follow this super-simple rule of thumb from wine educator Mark Oldman (*Oldman's Guide to Outsmarting Wine*): Fifteen minutes before serving time, take white wines out of the fridge, and pop the red ones in.

## ODD BEER NAMES

- Oliver's Hot Monkey Love
- Bourbon Barrel Lower da Boom
- Satan's Pony Amber Ale
- Butt Monkey Chimp Chiller Ale
- San Quentin Breakout Stout
- Aroma Borealis Herbal Cream Ale
- Kill Ugly Radio
- Old Knucklehead
- Money Shot Cream Ale
- 3 Stooges Beer
- Moose Drool
- Demon Sweat Imperial Red
- Monk in the Trunk
- Dead Frog Ale
- Tongue Buckler
- Bitter American
- Ninja vs. Unicorn

# THE CURSE OF THE BOY KING

The discovery of King Tut's tomb in 1922 is said to be the most important find ever in the field of Egyptology. But was there anything to the story of a curse that led to the death of the interlopers who dared disturb the resting place of the boy king? Or was that just an urban legend?

In November 1922, English archaeologist Howard Carter announced one of the world's greatest archaeological finds: the resting place of Tutankhamen, Egypt's fabled boy king. At nine years old, he was the youngest pharaoh ever. The tomb, discovered in the Valley of the Kings, was amazingly intact; it was one of the few Egyptian tombs to have escaped grave robbers. The furnishings and treasures were dazzling. In fact, the golden death mask that adorned the sarcophagus is purported to be the most renowned example of Egyptian art.

The boy king, who reigned from 1355 to 1344 B.C., was only 19 years old when he died. Until recently, the cause of his death was a mystery to historians. Many believed Tut had been murdered, but a recent CT scan of the mummy conducted by a team of researchers dispelled that possibility. According to experts, his death may have been from an infection that occurred as the result of a broken leg.

## THE CURSE THAT WON'T DIE

Another mystery surrounding the boy king is the alleged curse on anyone disturbing his resting place. That rumor can be traced back to the press. In 1923, shortly after the tomb was discovered, the man who endowed the expedition to locate Tut's tomb, Lord Carnarvon, was bitten on the cheek by a mosquito and died from a resulting infection. This was not an ominous event in itself, but when the lights of Cairo went out at the exact moment of his death, the press had a field day, and an urban legend was born. The legend continues to this day, especially each time Tut goes on tour.

# HISTORY'S GREAT ESCAPES

Men and women through the ages have risked great escapes to save their own lives and win their freedom.

## THE BALLAD OF MARY

Though the throne of England would elude her, Mary, Queen of Scots, struggled most of her life to assume the crown she believed to be her birthright. Imprisoned in remote Lochleven Castle in 1567 during a rebellion of Scottish nobles, her pleas for help were ignored by Queen Elizabeth of England and Queen Catherine de Medici, regent of France. In March 1568, Mary attempted to escape by disguising herself as a laundress and fleeing the castle's small island by boat. Her plan was thwarted when the boatmen, who were not part of the plot, noticed her beautiful hands and face and realized she was royalty. Mary managed to return to her cell without alerting her guards, however, and tried again with the aid of an orphan she befriended in the castle. On May 2, 1568, Mary escaped from the castle and rode to her freedom on a stolen horse—an exploit immortalized by Scottish poets, balladeers, and romantic novelist Sir Walter Scott. Her ultimate fate, however, was not as bright. She spent the last 19 years of her life imprisoned by her cousin, Queen Elizabeth I, until she was beheaded in 1587.

## THE WORLD'S GREATEST LOVER

Sentenced by a Venetian court to five years in prison in 1755 for Freemasonry, practicing magic, and numerous offenses of adultery, Giacomo Casanova was soon plotting his freedom. Incarcerated in a Vienna prison called "the Leads" for the lead coating its walls and roof, the young captive must have thought escape impossible. Casanova started work on a tunnel anyway, using an iron rod he found in the prison yard. Several months into the project, he was forced to move to another cell where he would be under close surveillance. Casanova managed to slip his tool to a monk named Balbi who was imprisoned in an adjacent cell. Hiding messages in the spines of books they were allowed to trade, he convinced the monk to dig a tunnel joining their cells. After digging a second tunnel from the monk's cell to the prison's roof, on the night of November 1, 1756, they used bed sheets as ropes to climb to an adjacent palace and used the iron rod to pry open several doors and reach the ground. Casanova fled Venice in a stolen gondola—the only prisoner to that time to carry out a successful escape from the Leads.

## UP, UP, AND AWAY, OVER THE IRON CURTAIN

In September 1979, Peter Strelzyk, Günter Wetzel, their wives, and four children dropped from the night sky onto a field in West Germany, flying a homemade hot-air balloon. Strelzyk and Wetzel built the balloon's platform and burners in one of their basements. Their wives sewed random pieces of fabric together to make the 75-foot-high balloon. A bid to escape communist East Germany during the days of the Berlin Wall, their famous flight was two years in the making, spanned 15 miles, and took 28 minutes to complete. Unsure whether they had reached freedom, the two families spent the next morning hiding in a barn. When they saw an Audi traveling down a nearby road, they realized they had reached the West.

 # Why Did the Nazis Keep a Record of the Holocaust?

The events of World War II were recorded to an extent far beyond that of preceding conflicts. Events were captured in print, photographs, and moving pictures. The most chilling of all was the exhaustive documentation of the Holocaust, much of it created by the very people who committed the crimes.

Knowledge of the Holocaust stems from many sources, the most compelling of which are the eyewitness testimonies of victims. But there is another source that helps confirm the extermination's unthinkable scale, as well as the fates of individuals. That source is the accounts kept by the Nazis themselves.

Seized by the liberating armies in the last days of the war, the documentation exists in various collections, but the bulk of the records have been under the care of the Red Cross for the last half-century. The files are extensive: millions upon millions of papers covering 16 miles of shelves. So why would a group of people intent on murder risk putting their activities in writing?

The answer may surprise you. In the opinion of Paul Shapiro, director of Holocaust studies at the United States Holocaust Memorial Museum, "They wanted to show they were getting the job done." Many accounts suggest that he may be correct.

## JUST A JOB: THE BUREAUCRACY OF THE DEVIL

A stereotypical but not entirely inaccurate image of the prewar German government is one of bureaucracy. Everything was documented, and paper authorizations were generated by the handful for the most mundane of tasks. This attitude extended into the war. The task of running an empire, even a despicable one, is complex, requiring extensive procedures and paper trails. Like many governments, Nazi Germany employed an array of middle managers who wanted to prove their efficiency. The only way an official could show he was performing up to par was to keep records.

Prisoners who were immediately executed had the least documentation, sometimes being reduced to a mere entry in the number of arrivals for the day. Individuals who stayed in the camps longer typically had more extensive records. Because of the sheer number of people involved—some 17 million in all—some startling documents survived, such as the original list of Jews transferred to safety in the factories of Oskar Schindler. Another file contains the records of Anne Frank.

## WHY WORRY?

For most of the war, the Nazis showed little compunction about documenting their activities. In their minds, why should they? To whom would they be accountable? After all, many thought the Third Reich would last a thousand years. In the closing months of the war, there was a slight reversal of this policy, and the commandants of some camps sought to destroy records and eliminate the remaining witnesses as the Allied forces closed in. Fortunately, they were not able to erase the record of their own atrocities.

Private memoirs of the Holocaust also exist. Participants at all levels wrote letters about their experiences, and some SS guards took photographs of the camps and inmates with their personal cameras. Some of the Nazi leadership was also prone to recording daily activities; Joseph Goebbels kept a journal throughout the war, viewing it as a "substitute for the confessional."

Much like Goebbels's diary, the official records of the Holocaust have become the unintentional confession of a Nazi machine that had uncountable crimes for which to answer. The archive exists in Bad Arolsen, Germany, and was opened to the online public in 2006. Survivors of the camps hope that its presence serves as a counterargument to those who inexplicably deny that the Holocaust ever happened, and as a reminder that humankind must never allow it to happen again.

# FROM THE VAULTS OF HISTORY

## AT LEAST THERE'S NOT A LIEN ON IT

The Leaning Tower of Pisa is a bell tower built more than 800 years ago in Pisa, Italy. Pisa was originally named Poseidonia, from a Greek word meaning "marshy land." Bonanno Pisano, the original architect, didn't think this was important information. In 1173, he decided to build a shallow foundation about three meters deep. Five years later, Bonanno realized that his structure was sinking on one side because he built upon a bed of dense clay. To attempt to solve the problem, he added two inches to the southern columns and thought no one would notice. People noticed. The third floor reached completion, and the job was halted.

In 1272, construction resumed under the guidance of architect Giovanni di Simone. He completed four more floors, built at an angle to compensate for the listing. But his remedy caused the tower to tilt in the other direction. In 1284, the job was halted again. In 1319, the Pisans completed the seventh floor. The bell tower was added in 1372, and then it was left to lean in peace until the 19th century.

In 1838, the foundation was dug out so visitors could see how it was built, which caused the tower to lean even more. Then in 1934, Benito Mussolini ordered the foundation to be reinforced with concrete. But the concrete was too heavy, and it sunk the tower further into the clay.

Since then, many projects have come and gone. The tower now stands nearly 185 feet tall, is estimated to weigh almost 16,000 tons, and leans at an angle of almost four degrees (about four meters off vertical).

## REALLY SNAIL-MAIL

The oldest message in a bottle that has ever been found spent 92 years and 229 days at sea. The bottle was released on April 25, 1914, in the Norwegian Sea northeast of the Shetland Islands of Scotland. On December 10, 2006, that same bottle was found only about a mile away from the spot where it first went into the water. A fisher named Mark Anderson of Bixter, on the Shetland Islands, rescued it.

## OLDER THAN DIRT

The oldest living animal in recorded history is a clam. Nicknamed Ming, for the time period in which it was born, the clam sat in the Atlantic Ocean off the coast of Iceland. Scientists counted the growth rings on the clam's shell to determine its age. Most clams live around 200 years if undisturbed, but Ming lived a lot longer—405 years.

# THE GREAT HUNGER

When the Irish potato crop failed in 1845, it caused a tragedy that devastated the nation for generations.

The Ireland of 1845 was a British colony where many of the people labored as tenant farmers for English landlords, raising grain and grazing cattle for export. To feed themselves, the Irish cultivated potatoes on tiny plots of land. Some historians assert that by the 1840s, half of Ireland's population of eight million ate nothing but potatoes. Then an unwelcome visitor—a mold called *Phytophthora infestans*—arrived from America. This "potato blight" rotted the precious tubers in the fields. Between 1845 and 1849—a period that became known, in Gaelic, as *An Gorta Mór*, "The Great Hunger"—an estimated one million Irish died of outright starvation or from the diseases that stalked in famine's wake. Another 1–1.5 million left their homeland in desperation. Some went to England or to British colonies such as Australia. Many others chose to cut their ties to the British Empire and cross the Atlantic to settle in the United States—where they played a crucial role in building America. Seventy years after the famine ended, Ireland's population was only about half of what it had been in 1845.

The British government organized some relief efforts, but the effort was a classic case of too little, too late. Worse was the fact that even at the height of the famine, the Emerald Isle still teemed with food—for export to England! The fiercely independent, mostly Catholic Irish had long resented British domination of their island, but the timid British response to the famine fueled a new spirit of rebellion that culminated in Ireland's full independence in 1937.

# A FEW WHO SAVED MANY

During World War II, many individuals worked to save Jews from extermination by the Nazis. Here are four individuals whose courage and moral fortitude saved thousands.

## RAOUL WALLENBERG

Wallenberg was a Swedish diplomat stationed in Budapest who saved more than 100,000 Hungarian Jews from July to December 1944. He designed, issued, and personally distributed some 4,500 "protective passports" that gave Jewish holders perceived safe passage to Sweden under the protection of the Swedish Crown. Wallenberg issued at least another 12,000 passports. When acting personally, he often handed the passports to Jews aboard trains awaiting deportation and convinced authorities they were to be released under his protection. He also established havens for Jews in Budapest homes, dubbed "Swedish houses" because they flew the Swedish flag and were declared Swedish territory. Finally, he used diplomatic and moral pressure to prevent the liquidation of the Jewish

ghettos in Budapest. On January 17, 1945, Wallenberg was arrested by Soviet agents and never seen again. In 2000, the Russians admitted his wrongful imprisonment and reported that he died in captivity in 1947.

## YVONNE NÈVEJEAN

Nèvejean headed the Oeuvre Nationale de l'Enfance (ONE), a Belgian agency supervising children's homes. Funded by underground Jewish organizations and the Belgian government-in-exile, Nèvejean rescued more than 4,000 Jewish children by providing them with new identities, ration cards, and places of permanent refuge in private homes and institutions. She also arranged for the release of a group of children taken by the Gestapo to an internment camp to be readied for deportation. Children rescued by Nèvejean became known as "Yvonne's children."

## SUGIHARA (SEMPO) CHIUNE

Sugihara was the Japanese consul general in Kovno at the time of the Soviet invasion of Lithuania. When the Soviets ordered all foreign delegations out of Kovno in July 1940, Sugihara asked for a 20-day extension and, in defiance of explicit orders from the Japanese Foreign Ministry, issued transit visas to Polish and Lithuanian Jews seeking to escape both the Nazis and the Soviets. Through August 1940, he and his wife, Yukiko, worked day and night signing papers for Jews waiting in long lines around the Japanese consulate building. In a race against time, he provided lifesaving documents for more than 6,000 "Sugihara Survivors," signing papers and shoving them through the train window even as he was leaving Kovno. "I should follow my conscience," he said at the time. "I cannot allow these people to die, people who had come to me for help with death staring them in the eyes."

## OSKAR SCHINDLER

Immortalized in the film *Schindler's List*, Schindler was a German businessman and Nazi Party member who entertained and bribed German Army and SS officials in Poland to obtain contracts and Jewish labor for an enamel kitchenware factory in Krakow he had taken over from a Jewish firm. Awakened to the fact by his Jewish accountant that work in his factory meant survival for Jews, Schindler hired more Jews than he needed, convincing SS officials with bribes that he needed their "essential" skills. In all, he saved more than 1,300 "Schindlerjuden" by employing them in his various factories. When Nazis who elected to ignore Schindler's "arrangement" put scores of Schindler workers onto a train headed for Auschwitz, Oskar came up with additional bribes, and had the workers released into his custody. "If you saw a dog going to be crushed under a car," he said later of his actions, "wouldn't you help him?"

# HISTORY'S SHORTEST WARS

Here are some of the shortest conflicts in history.

**Anglo-Zanzibar War (9:02–9:40 A.M., August 27, 1896, Great Britain versus Zanzibar):** The British liked it when the Sultan of Zanzibar (an island off modern Tanzania) engaged in battles. When a new sultan named Khalid bin Barghash refused to, the Royal Navy gave Zanzibar a taste of British anger. Bin Barghash tapped out after just 38 minutes of shelling in what is the shortest recorded war.

**Spanish-American War (April 25–August 12, 1898, United States versus Spain):** Spain once had an empire, some of which was very near Florida. After months of tension, the battleship USS *Maine* blew up in Havana harbor. Though no one knew why it exploded, the United States declared war anyway. A few months later, Spain had lost Cuba, Guam, the Philippines, and Puerto Rico.

**Nazi-Polish War (September 1–October 6, 1939, Nazi Germany and Soviet Union versus Poland):** After Russian and German negotiators signed a secret agreement in August for the division of Poland, the Nazis invaded in vicious armored thrusts with heavy air attacks. Polish forces fought with uncommon valor, but their strategic position was impossible. Russian troops entered from the east on September 17, and Poland became the first European nation conquered in World War II.

**Nazi-Danish War (4:15–9:20 A.M., April 9, 1940, Nazi Germany versus Denmark):** Arguably the biggest mismatch of World War II (unless one counts Germany's invasion of Luxembourg). Sixteen Danish soldiers died before the Danish government ordered the resistance to cease.

**Suez/Sinai War (October 29–November 6, 1956, Israel, Britain, and France versus Egypt):** The Egyptians decided to nationalize the Suez Canal, which seems logical today given that the Suez is entirely in Egypt. British and French companies operating the canal didn't agree. The Israelis invaded by land, the British and French by air and sea. The invaders won a complete military victory, but the rest of world got so mad at them that they withdrew.

**Six-Day War (June 5–10, 1967, Israel versus Egypt, Syria, and Jordan):** Israelis launched a sneak attack on the Egyptians, destroying the Egyptian air force on its airfields and sending the Egyptians reeling back toward the Suez Canal. Jordanians attacked the Israelis and immediately regretted it. The Israelis attacked Syria and seized Golan Heights.

**Yom Kippur War (October 6–25, 1973, Egypt and Syria versus Israel):** Egyptians and Syrians, still annoyed and embarrassed over the Six-Day War, attacked Israelis on a national religious holiday. Israeli forces were caught napping at first but soon regained the upper hand—they struck within artillery range of Damascus and crossed the Suez Canal. The United Nations' ceasefire came as a major relief to all involved, even the Israelis, who had no desire to administer Cairo and Damascus.

**Soccer War (July 15–19, 1969, El Salvador versus Honduras):** Immigration was the core issue, specifically the forced expulsion of some 60,000 Salvadorean illegal immigrants from Honduras. When a soccer series between the two Central American nations fueled tensions, a bloody yet inconclusive war followed.

# Why Didn't the Vikings Stay in North America?

Because they weren't particularly good guests, and the Native Americans threw them out. According to ancient Norse sagas that were written in the 13th century, Leif Eriksson was the first Viking to set foot in North America.

After wintering at the place we now call Newfoundland in the year 1000, Leif went home. In 1004, his brother Thorvald led the next expedition, composed of 30 men, and met the natives for the first time. The Vikings attacked and killed eight of the nine native men they encountered. A greater force retaliated, and Thorvald was killed. His men then returned home.

Six years later, a larger expedition of Viking men, women, and livestock set up shop in North America. They lasted two years, according to the sagas. The Vikings traded with the locals initially, but they soon started fighting with them and were driven off. There may have been one further attempt at a Newfoundland settlement by Leif and Thorvald's sister, Freydis.

In 1960, Norse ruins of the appropriate age were found in L'Anse aux Meadows, Newfoundland, by Norwegian couple Helge and Anne Stine Ingstad. The Vikings had been there, all right. Excavations over the next seven years uncovered large houses and ironworks where nails and rivets were made, as well as woodworking areas. Also found were spindlewhorls, weights that were used when spinning thread; this implies that women were present, which suggests the settlement was more than a vacation camp. The ruins don't reveal why the Vikings left, but they do confirm what the old sagas claimed: The Vikings were in North America.

The sagas say that the settlers fought with the local *Skraelings*, a Norse word meaning "natives," until the *Skraelings* came at them in large enough numbers to force the Vikings out.

This sounds plausible, given the reputation of the Vikings—they'd been raiding Europe for centuries—and the Eriksson family's history of violence. Erik the Red, the father of Leif, founded a Greenland colony because he'd been thrown out of Iceland for murder, and Erik's father had been expelled from Norway for the same reason. Would you want neighbors like them?

## A BRIEF HISTORY OF UNDERWEAR

- The earliest and most simple undergarment was the loincloth—a long strip of material worn between the legs and around the waist. King Tutankhamen was buried with 145 of them, but the style didn't go out with the Egyptians. Loincloths are still worn in many Asian and African cultures.

- Men in the Middle Ages wore loose, trouserlike undergarments called *braies*, which one stepped into and tied around the waist and legs about mid-calf. To facilitate urination, braies were fitted with a codpiece, a flap that buttoned or tied closed.

- Medieval women wore a close-fitting undergarment called a *chemise*, and corsets began to appear in the 18th century. Early versions of the corset were designed to flatten a woman's bustline, but by the late 1800s, corsets were reconstructed to give women an exaggerated hourglass shape.

- In the late 1800s and early 1900s, chastity was a big concern for married or committed couples. During that time, many inventors received patents for "security underwear" for men. These devices were meant to assure "masculine chastity." They ensured that men refrained from sexual relations with anyone other than the person with the key to open that particular device.

- Around 1920, as women became more involved in sports such as tennis and bicycling, loose, comfortable bloomers replaced corsets as the undergarment of choice. The constricting corset soon fell out of favor altogether.

## Were There Female Druids?

Absolutely. The Celts—the culture that produced druids—were far less gender-biased than their Greek and Roman neighbors. In Celtic societies, women could buy or inherit property, assume leadership, wage war, divorce men, and, yes, become druids.

Druids were the leaders—spiritually, intellectually, and sometimes politically—of the Celts. Because they did not use writing, we don't know exactly what druids (or their followers) believed, or what they taught. From ancient stories, we've learned that they were well-educated and served as judges, scientists, teachers, priests, and doctors. Some even led their tribes.

At one time, Celtic tribes covered most of Europe, and their druids embodied wisdom and authority. In the ensuing centuries, however, druids have gotten a bad rap, due to lurid tales of human sacrifice that may or may not be true. Most of the bad-mouthing came from enemies of the Celts, so take what they said with the proverbial grain of salt.

Greek writers like Plutarch and Romans such as Tacitus described femme druids as priestesses, prophets, and oracles. Several ancient authors mention holy women living on island sanctuaries, either alone or alongside male druids.

Irish tales are full of druids, some of them women. They helped win battles by transforming trees into warriors. They conjured up storms and diseases, and sometimes they hid children from murderous fathers. In the Irish epic *Cattle Raid of Cooley*, a beautiful young druid named Fidelma foretells victory for the hero Cúchulainn. Saint Patrick met female druids, and Saint Bridget, by some accounts the daughter of a druid, may have been a druid herself before converting to Christianity.

The Celts knew what the rest of the world has slowly come to realize: Women can wield power as wisely—or as cruelly—as men.

# CURIOUS WORLD CURRENCIES

Paper, coins, and plastic are what we use as money today, but that wasn't always the case. Throughout history, people have used various animals, vegetables, and minerals to conduct business.

Cows represent the oldest of all forms of money, dating from as early as 9000 B.C. The words "capital," "chattels," and "cattle" have a common root, and the word "pecuniary" (meaning "financial") comes from pecus, the Latin word for cattle. But cattle weren't the only livestock used as legal tender: Until well into the 20th century, the Kirghiz (a Turkic ethnic group found primarily in Kyrgyzstan) used horses for large exchanges, sheep for lesser trades, and lambskins for barters that required only small change.

Cowry shells—marine snails found chiefly in tropical regions—were the medium of exchange used in China around 1200 B.C. These shells were so widely traded that their pictograph became the symbol for money in the written language. The earliest metallic money in China were cowries made of bronze or copper.

Throughout history, salt and pepper have been used as money, both for their value as seasonings and preservatives and for their importance in religious ceremonies. In ancient Rome, salt was used as money, and the Latin word for salt (sal) is the root of the word "salary." Roman workers were paid with salt, hence the expression "worth one's salt." Pepper was also used as a form of payment. During the Middle Ages in England, rent could be paid in peppercorns.

The largest form of money is the 12-foot limestone coins from the Micronesian island of Yap. A coin's value was determined by its size. Displaying a large coin outside your home was a sign of status and prestige. Because of the coins' size and immobility, islanders would often trade only promises of ownership instead of actual coins. Approximately 6,800 coins still exist around the island, though the U.S. dollar is now the official currency.

# Who Betrayed Anne Frank?

Anne Frank and her family thwarted Nazis for two years, hiding in Amsterdam until someone blew their cover.

Annelies Marie Frank was born in Frankfurt am Main, Germany, on June 12, 1929. Perhaps the most well known victim of the Holocaust, she was one of approximately 1.5 million Jewish children killed by the Nazis. Her diary chronicling her experience in Amsterdam was discovered in the Franks' secret hiding place by friends of the family and first published in 1947. Translated into more than 60 languages, *Anne Frank: The Diary of a Young Girl* has sold 30 million copies and is one of the most read books in the world.

The diary was given to Anne on her 13th birthday, just weeks before she went into hiding. Her father, Otto Frank, moved his family and four friends into a secret annex of rooms above his office at 263 Prinsengracht on July 6, 1942. They relied on friends and trustworthy business associates, who risked their own lives to help them. Anne poignantly wrote her thoughts, yearnings, and descriptions of life in the secret annex in her diary, revealing a vibrant, intelligent young woman struggling to retain her ideals in the most dire of circumstances.

On August 4, 1944, four or five Dutch Nazi collaborators under the command of an Austrian Nazi police investigator entered the building and arrested the Franks and their friends. The family was deported to Auschwitz, where they were separated and sent to different camps. Anne and her sister, Margot, were sent to Bergen-Belsen, where they both died of typhus a few weeks before liberation. Anne was 15 years old. Otto Frank was the only member of the group to survive the war.

Dutch police, Nazi hunters, and historians have attempted to identify the person who betrayed the Franks. Searching for clues, the Netherlands Institute for War Documentation (NIWD) has examined records on Dutch collaboration with the Nazis, the letters of Otto Frank, and police transcripts dating from the 1940s. Nazi hunter Simon Wiesenthal also questioned the arresting Nazi officer after the war, but he could not identify who informed on the Franks. For decades suspicion centered on Willem Van Maaren, who worked in the warehouse attached to the Franks' hiding place, but two police investigations found no evidence against him.

Two recent theories have been offered about who betrayed the Franks. British author Carol Anne Lee believes it was Anton Ahlers, a business associate of Otto's who was a petty thief and member of the Dutch Nazi movement. Lee argues that Ahlers informed the Nazis to collect the bounty paid to Dutch civilians who exposed Jews. She suggests he may have split the reward with Maarten Kuiper, a friend of Ahlers who was one of the Dutch Nazi collaborators who raided the secret annex. Ahlers was jailed for collaboration with the Nazis after the war, and members of his own family, including his son, have said they believe he was guilty of informing on the Franks.

Austrian writer Melissa Müller believes that a cleaning lady, Lena Hartog, who also worked in the warehouse, reported the Franks because she feared that if they were discovered, her husband, an employee of Otto Frank, would be deported for aiding Jews.

The NIWD has studied the arguments of both writers and examined the evidence supporting their theories. Noting that all the principals involved in the case are no longer living, it concluded that neither theory could be proved.

# ON A ROLL: TOILET PAPER

Like pasta and gunpowder, toilet paper was invented in China. Paper—made from pulped bamboo and cotton rags—was also invented by the Chinese, although Egyptians had already been using papyrus plants to make writing surfaces for thousands of years. Still, it wasn't until 1391, almost 1,600 years after the invention of paper, that the Ming Dynasty Emperor first used toilet paper. By 1393, the imperial court was going through 720,000 sheets annually, at a massive two by three feet each.

Toilet paper didn't reach the United States until 1857 when the Gayetty Firm introduced "medicated" paper. Prior to the industrial revolution later that century, many amenities were available only to the wealthy. But in 1890, Scott Paper Company brought toilet paper to the masses. The company employed new manufacturing techniques to introduce perforated sheets. In 1942, Britain's St. Andrew's Paper Mill invented two-ply sheets. Two-ply sheets are not just two single-ply sheets stuck together; each ply in a two-ply sheet is thinner than a single-ply sheet. The first "moist" toilet paper—Cottonelle Fresh Rollwipes—appeared in 2001.

What was the rest of the world doing? Some pretty creative stuff! Romans soaked sponges in saltwater and attached them to the end of sticks. There is little information about what happened when the stick poked through the sponge, but the Romans were a hearty, expansionist people and probably conquered another country for spite. Medieval farmers used balls of hay. American pioneers used corncobs. Leaves have always been a popular alternative to toilet paper. Inuit people favor Tundra moss. Of all people, the Vikings seemed the most sensible, using wool.

# GEOGRAPHIC ODDITIES

**Atacama Desert (Chile):** This 600-mile stretch of coastal desert is so lung-searingly dry that if you die there, your corpse will barely decay. In some parts, no rainfall has been recorded by humans, but a million people still live in the region.

**Blue Hole of Belize (Lighthouse Reef off Belize, Central America):** Sixty miles out from Belize City, there's a circular reef in the shallow water about a quarter mile across, encasing a perfectly round, 400-foot-deep pool of midnight blue.

**Cliffs of Moher (County Clare, Ireland):** Here you can be rained on from above and below. The sheer cliffs rise more than 600 feet above sea level, and the surf's force is violent enough to send spray all the way to the top. When it's raining, one gets the stereo effect of being thoroughly drenched from both ends.

**North Pacific Gyre Trash Vortex (Pacific Ocean):** About a third of the way from California to Hawaii, a swirling ocean current collects garbage and doesn't easily let it go. This patch, now the size of Texas, consists mostly of floating plastic debris such as bottles and grocery bags. Unfortunately, as the pieces degrade, birds and fish eat them and die.

**Punalu'u Black Sand Beach (Hawaii):** Some places have beautiful beaches with sand that's white, or various shades of tan, or maybe even dark gray. Rarely, however, does one see sand that's as black as charcoal. The peculiar sand of Punalu'u is made of lava that exploded when it hit the water and has since been ground very fine. If that isn't strange enough, there are freshwater springs beneath the saltwater surf.

**Uluru (Northern Territory, Australia):** Formerly known as Ayers Rock, this enormous rusty sandstone monolith sticks up more than 1,100 feet from the desert floor and is about two miles wide. The rock is spiritually sacred to the Anangu (Australian Aborigines).

**Uyuni Salt Flats (southern Bolivia):** Roughly 25 times the size of the Bonneville Salt Flats in the United States, this saline landscape covers more than 4,000 square miles of Bolivia at an altitude of 12,500 feet. Because of brine just below the surface, any crack in the salt soon repairs itself.

# THEN AND NOW: ANCIENT CITIES

In the ancient world, it took far fewer people to make a great city. Some didn't survive, but others have flourished. With the understanding that ancient population estimates are necessarily approximate, here are the fates of some great metropolises:

**Memphis (now the ruins of Memphis, Egypt):** By 3100 B.C., this Pharaonic capital bustled with an estimated 30,000 people. Today it has none—but modern Cairo, 12 miles north, is home to an estimated 12 million people.

**Ur (now the ruins of Ur, Iraq):** Sumer's great ancient city once stood near the Euphrates with a peak population of 65,000 around 2030 B.C. The Euphrates has meandered about ten miles northeast, and Ur now has a population of zero.

**Alexandria (now El-Iskandariya, Egypt):** Built on an ancient Egyptian village site near the Nile Delta's west end, Alexander the Great's city once held a tremendous library. In its heyday, it may have held 250,000 people; today more than 3,300,000 people call it home.

**Babylon (now the ruins of Babylon, Iraq):** Babylon may have twice been the largest city in the world, in about 1700 B.C. and 500 B.C.—perhaps with up to 200,000 people in the latter case. Now, it's windblown dust and faded splendor.

**Athens (Greece):** In classical times, this powerful city-state stood miles from the coast but was never a big place— something like 30,000 residents during the 300s B.C. It now reaches the sea with about 3,000,000 residents.

**Rome (Italy):** With the rise of its empire, ancient Rome became a city of more than 500,000 and the center of Western civilization. Though that mantle moved on to other cities, Rome now has around 3,000,000 people.

**Xi'an (China):** This longtime dynastic capital, famed for its terra-cotta warriors but home to numerous other antiquities, reached 400,000 people by A.D. 637. Its nearly 8,000,000 people make it as important a city now as it was then.

**Constantinople (now Istanbul, Turkey):** First colonized by Greeks in the 1200s B.C., this city of fame was made Emperor Constantine the Great's eastern imperial Roman capital with 300,000 people. Today, it is Turkey's largest city with around 14,000,000 people.

**Baghdad (Iraq):** Founded around A.D. 762, this center of Islamic culture and faith was perhaps the first city to house more than 1,000,000 people.

**Tenochtitlán (now Mexico City, Mexico):** Founded in A.D. 1325, this island-built Aztec capital had more than 200,000 inhabitants within a century. Most of the surrounding lake has been drained over the years. A staggering 19,000,000 souls call modern Mexico City home.

**Carthage (now the ruins of Carthage, Tunisia):** Phoenician seafarers from the Levant founded this great trade city in 814 B.C. Before the Romans obliterated it in 146 B.C., its population may have reached 700,000. Today, it sits in empty silence ten miles from modern Tunis—population 2,000,000.

 # ODD AND UNUSUAL STRUCTURES

### SEDLEC OSSUARY: THE SKELETON SANCTUARY
A chandelier made of every bone in the human skeleton, a heap of 14th century skulls with arrow wounds, and a skull and crossbones atop a tower all make the little chapel known as the Sedlec Ossuary a most unusual church.

Located just outside the medieval silver-mining center of Kutna Hora, Czech Republic, in a suburb now called Sedlec, the chapel was predated by a cemetery made famous in 1278 after a church official sprinkled it with soil from the

Holy Land. The chapel was built in 1400, but by 1511, the cemetery was so overcrowded that bones were dug up and stored inside. In 1870, a woodcarver named Frantisek Rindt was hired to organize the bones of the 40,000 people stashed in the ossuary, so he decided to assemble them into a fantastic assortment of altars, sculptures, and other furnishings and decorations.

## DANCING HOUSE OF PRAGUE: A BUILDING THAT BOOGIES
Originally named the "Astaire and Rogers" building after the famous dance duo, the modern building's swaying towers suggest a dancing couple. The building, which houses a popular restaurant, was designed by architects Vlado Milunic and Frank Gehry and built in the mid-1990s. Set in a traditional neighborhood of Baroque, Gothic, and Art Nouveau buildings, the crunched appearance of the Dancing House inspired great local controversy when first proposed.

## BANGKOK ROBOT BUILDING: BANKING ON ROBOTS
The world's first robot-shaped building houses the United Overseas Bank headquarters in Bangkok, Thailand, and was designed to reflect the hope that robots will someday release humanity from the burden of drudgework. Designed by Dr. Sumet Jumsai and built mostly of native materials, the energy-efficient, 20-story "robot" includes a day-care center and an 18th floor dining room with a sweeping view of the city. The building, finished in 1986, is complete with reflective glass eyes, lightning rod "antennae," and bright blue walls.

## POLAND'S CROOKED HOUSE: WAVY-WALLED WONDER
Tipsy bar patrons who wander outside the Crooked House in Sopot, Poland, may rightly wonder if their eyes deceive

them. But whether viewed with or without an alcoholic haze, the curving facade is purposely out-of-kilter, and its green shingles are intended to look like the scales of a dragon. The building is home to several pubs, coffee shops, and other businesses.

## SHIGERU BAN'S HOUSES OF CARDBOARD

In the 1980s, Japanese architect Shigeru Ban began making buildings from cardboard tubes because he felt good structure should be affordable to anyone and that a new kind of architecture could arise from so-called "weak materials." Ban used his idea to develop inexpensive yet durable shelters for refugees from natural disasters. He has also designed spectacular buildings from what he calls "improved wood." One of the most famous is his Nomadic Museum, made out of approximately 150 shipping containers that can be sent and reassembled anywhere in the world. Inside, it features giant curtains made from thousands of recycled tea bags.

## HOUSTON BEER CAN HOUSE: THE SIX-PACK SHACK

The ultimate in recycling projects, John Milkovisch's Houston home, which is covered with siding made from smashed beer cans, has proven that even a six-pack-a-day habit can be eco-friendly. That's about what it took to provide materials over the course of 20 years. After his retirement from the railroad in 1968, Milkovisch started the project just to have something to do and drank some 40,000 cans of Coors, Bud Light, and Texas Pride to create his unique habitat. For a bit of flair, he added wind chime curtains made from pulltabs and arranged horizontal rows of cans to provide decorative fences.

## SOUTH KOREA TOILET HOUSE: THE POTTY HOUSE

South Korean lawmaker Sim Jae-Duck is flushed with pride over the house he built in Suwon in 2007—the home is shaped like a giant toilet. Sim Jae-Duck, who built the home for a meeting of the World Toilet Association, said he hoped to persuade people to think of toilets not just as a "place of defecation" but also a "place of culture." The two-story home is outfitted with four actual toilets, including one encased in motion-sensitive glass that fogs up for privacy. The house's staircase spirals where the drain would be if the structure were actually a toilet. The 4,520-square foot house sits on the site of Sim Jae-Duck's former home, which was tanked for the new project.

## WHERE YOU'D LEAST EXPECT IT

- A stolen painting by Mexican artist Tamayo was retrieved from an unlikely place: the trash. Out on a stroll, Elizabeth Gibson spotted it nestled among some garbage. After finding the painting posted on a Web site four years later, Gibson received a share of the one million dollars it fetched at Sotheby's.

- John Wilkes Booth's body is buried in a Baltimore cemetery, but his third, fourth, and fifth vertebrae can be found on display in the National Health and Medicine Museum in Washington, D.C. They were removed for investigation after he was shot and killed while on the run following Lincoln's assassination.

- The pathologist who performed Albert Einstein's autopsy, Dr. Thomas Harvey, kept a pretty major souvenir: Einstein's brain. Thirty years postmortem, the brain segments were found in the doctor's Kansas home, stored in a pair of mason jars.

- Normally on display at the Elvis After Dark Museum, a handgun once owned by the King was stolen during a ceremony on the 30th anniversary of his death. Soon thereafter, the missing gun was found stashed inside a mucky portable toilet only yards from where the gun's exhibit case sat.

- Egypt, which receives less rainfall than most places on Earth, doesn't seem like the kind of place where you'd find sea creatures. Yet, it was there that geologists discovered the nearly complete skeleton of a Basilosaurus, a prehistoric whale. During the whale's lifetime, 40 million years ago, Egypt's Wadi Hitan desert was underwater.

- *Femme nue couchée*, a racy female nude painted by Gustave Courbet in the 19th century, turned up on a Slovakian doctor's wall in 2000, nearly six decades after it disappeared during World War II. It was believed to have been stolen by members of the Russian Red Army, but the country doctor claimed that he received the art in payment for services rendered.

# UNUSUAL U.S. ATTRACTIONS

### FORBIDDEN GARDENS, KATY, TEXAS
Built by a Hong Kong tycoon as a testament to Chinese history, this Houston-area attraction features a one-third-scale model of one of China's greatest archeological finds: Emperor Qin's tomb and its resident army of 6,000 terra-cotta soldiers. The Gardens also include an elaborate model of the Forbidden City.

## WORLD'S THIRD-LARGEST FIRE HYDRANT, BEAUMONT, TEXAS

Painted white with black spots to promote the video release of Disney's *101 Dalmatians*, this 24-foot-tall hydrant was a gift from the movie studio to the Fire Museum of Texas, where it is on permanent display. The waterworks within the mottled shell are capable of blasting 25 gallons a second. Just two years after the Beaumont hydrant was erected, a 29½-foot fire hydrant was unveiled in Elm Creek, Manitoba, Canada, taking over honors as the world's largest.

## CARHENGE, ALLIANCE, NEBRASKA

To memorialize his father, engineer Jim Reinders organized a project that became the stuff of legend: the construction of a scale model of Stonehenge using junked cars instead of slabs of stone. With the help of a backhoe, Reinders and his kin put together this lasting tribute to a much more mysterious landmark halfway around the world.

## FOUNTAIN OF YOUTH, ST. AUGUSTINE, FLORIDA

The site of a natural spring that Spanish explorer Juan Ponce de León mistook for the legendary Fountain of Youth in 1513 is now a kitschy attraction with touristy diversions of all kinds. The spring's water is free for the taking, but you have to buy the souvenir bottle in which to take it home.

## WORLD'S LARGEST BALL OF PAINT, ALEXANDRIA, INDIANA

In 1977, Mike Carmichael started applying layer after layer of paint to an ordinary baseball. Since then, the ball has seen an average of two coats a day, earning the title "The World's Largest Ball of Paint." After more than 20,000 coats, the ball measures about 3 feet in diameter and weighs well over 1,300 pounds.

## ORIGINAL AMERICAN KAZOO COMPANY FACTORY AND MUSEUM, EDEN, NEW YORK

The Original American Kazoo Company began cranking out those crazy kazoos in 1916 and is now the world's only maker of metal kazoos. At the museum, visitors can experience the entire kazoo-making process and view the original factory equipment. Displays include rare silver and gold kazoos, as well as kazoos of many shapes and sizes. A big metal kazoo—said to be the world's largest—adorns the roof of the museum.

# SILLY CITY NAMES

- Boring, Maryland
- Bread Loaf, Vermont
- Ding Dong, Texas
- Energy, Illinois
- Hot Coffee, Mississippi
- Intercourse, Pennsylvania
- Lizard Lick, North Carolina
- Monkeys Eyebrow, Kentucky
- Santa Claus, Indiana
- Tightwad, Missouri
- Waterproof, Louisiana
- Why, Arizona
- Yum Yum, Tennessee

# FRESNO'S UNDERGROUND GARDENS

Italians have always had a knack for ingenuity, and Baldassare Forestiere was no exception, handcrafting a complex network of underground gardens when he realized his plot of land couldn't grow wine grapes.

In 1905, Baldassare Forestiere and his brother arrived in California's San Joaquin Valley. They had come to "the land of opportunity" to seek their fortune by growing fruit trees. Unfortunately, the land they bought was a lemon—but not the kind you can harvest and sell. Instead of giving up after buying land that was totally unfit to grow much of anything, Forestiere combined his knowledge of farming with his fascination with Roman architecture and decided to go underground.

The cool cellarlike tunnels Forestiere dug provided naturally air-conditioned rooms to beat the oppressive Fresno heat. And with access to groundwater and enough sunlight, he figured he might actually be able to grow something underground.

Forestiere first built a home that provided shelter from Fresno's hot summers, and for the next 40 years, he kept on digging. Shovel by shovel, he and his brother carved their worthless farmland into a maze of underground caverns where their dreams of plant cultivation were realized.

By 1923, they had carved out more than ten acres of tunnels, rooms, patios, and grottos in the rocky soil—all by hand.

They dug bed niches, bath alcoves, peepholes, stairways, grape arboretums, gardens, and holes that reached up through the bedrock so that trees growing beneath could get sunlight. Forestiere's underground home even had a parlor with a fireplace.

Visitors can still tour Forestiere's underground universe. The (under)grounds welcome visitors and are taken care of by Forestiere's relatives.

# TOP-SECRET LOCATIONS

There are plenty of stories of secret government facilities hidden in plain sight, where all sorts of strange tests take place, far away from the general public. Many of the North American top-secret government places have been (at least partially) declassified, allowing the average person to visit.

### TITAN MISSILE SILO

Just a little south of Tucson, Arizona, lies the Sonoran Desert, a barren, desolate area where nothing seems to be happening. That's exactly why, during the Cold War, the U.S. government hid an underground Titan Missile silo there.

Inside the missile silo, one of dozens that once littered the area, a Titan 2 Missile could be armed and launched in just under 90 seconds. Until it was finally abandoned in the 1990s, the government manned the silo 24 hours a day, with every member being trained to "turn the key" and launch the missile at a moment's notice. Today, the silo is open to the public as the Titan Missile Museum. Visitors can take a look at one of the few remaining Titan 2 missiles in existence, still sitting on the launch pad (relax, it's been disarmed). Folks with extra dough can also spend the night inside the silo and play the role of one of the crew members assigned to prepare to launch the missile at a moment's notice.

## PEANUT ISLAND

You wouldn't think a sunny place called Peanut Island, located near Palm Beach, Florida, could hold many secrets. Yet in December 1961, the U.S. Navy came to the island on a secret mission to create a fallout shelter for then-President John F. Kennedy and his family. The shelter was completed, but it was never used and was all but forgotten when the Cold War ended. Today, the shelter is maintained by the Palm Beach Maritime Museum, which conducts weekend tours of the space.

## WRIGHT-PATTERSON AIR FORCE BASE

If you believe that aliens crash-landed in Roswell, New Mexico, in the summer of 1947, then you need to make a trip out to Ohio's Wright-Patterson Air Force Base. That's because, according to legend, the UFO crash debris and possibly the aliens (both alive and dead) were shipped to the base as part of a government cover-up. Some say all that debris is still there, hidden away in an underground bunker beneath the mysterious Hanger 18.

While most of the Air Force Base is off-limits to the general public, you can go on a portion of the base to visit the National Museum of the U.S. Air Force, filled with amazing artifacts tracing the history of flight. But don't bother to ask any of the museum personnel how to get to Hanger 18—the official word is that the hanger does not exist.

## AREA 51

Located in the middle of the desert in southern Nevada lies possibly the world's best-known top-secret location: Area 51. If you've read a story about high-tech flying machines—either ours or extraterrestrial—chances are Area 51 was mentioned. That's because the government has spent years denying the base's existence, despite satellite photos showing otherwise. In fact, it was not until a lawsuit filed by government employees against the base that the government finally admitted the base did in fact exist.

If you want to find out what's going on inside Area 51, you're out of luck. While the dirt roads leading up to the base are technically public property, the base itself is very firmly not open for tours—if an unauthorized visitor so much as sets one toe over the boundary line, he or she is subject to arrest or worse.

## LOS ALAMOS NATIONAL LABORATORY

Until recently, the U.S. government refused to acknowledge the Los Alamos National Laboratory's existence. But in the early 1940s, the lab was created near Los Alamos, New Mexico, to develop the first nuclear weapons in what would become known as the Manhattan Project. Back then, the facility was so top secret it didn't even have a name. It was simply referred to as Site Y. No matter what it was called, the lab produced two nuclear bombs, nicknamed Little Boy and Fat Man—bombs that would be dropped on Hiroshima and Nagasaki, effectively ending World War II. Today, tours of portions of the facility can be arranged through the Lab's Public Affairs Department.

## FORT KNOX

It is the stuff that legends are made of: A mythical building filled with over 4,700 tons of gold, stacked up and piled high to the ceiling. But this is no fairytale—the gold really does exist, and it resides inside Fort Knox.

Since 1937, the U.S. Department of the Treasury's Bullion Depository has been storing the gold inside Fort Knox on a massive military campus that stretches across three counties in north-central Kentucky. Parts of the campus are open for tours, including the General George Patton Museum. But don't think you're going to catch a glimpse of that shiny stuff—visitors are not permitted to go through the gate or enter the building.

## THE EIFFEL TOWER

- Gustave Eiffel designed his monument to the French Revolution in 1887 as a grand entranceway to the 1889 International Exposition in Paris.

- Eiffel and his crew of 300 workers assembled the tower's 18,000 pieces of iron in two years, two months, and five days. They came in under budget and on time for the start of the fair.

- Every seven years, at least 25 workers use approximately 60 tons of paint to rustproof the tower.

- On a clear day, a person at the top of the Eiffel Tower can see about 42 miles in every direction.

- In just one year, the tower recouped nearly the entire cost of its construction—thanks to elevator ticket sales. The tower was one of the first tall structures in the world to use passenger elevators.

- The Eiffel Tower stands 989 feet tall and weighs approximately 10,000 tons.

- On the four sides of the tower, the names of 72 famous French scientists and engineers are engraved to honor their national contributions.

- There are 2.5 million rivets (short metal pins) in the Eiffel Tower.

- There are 1,665 steps to the top of the tower.

- Heat from the sun can cause the tower to expand up to three-fourths of an inch. During the cold winter months, the tower shrinks approximately six inches.

# UNEXPLAINED PHENOMENA

## THE PHILADELPHIA EXPERIMENT

On October 28, 1943, the USS *Eldridge* was allegedly made invisible for a brief moment as it sat in a naval shipyard in Philadelphia. Inexplicably, it had not only vanished but also teleported; at the same instant, it was witnessed at the U.S. naval base in Norfolk, Virginia. The event, which has never been factually substantiated but has been sworn as true by eyewitnesses and other believers for decades, is said to have been part of a U.S. military endeavor called the Philadelphia Experiment, or Project Rainbow. Legend has it that some of the crew onboard the USS *Eldridge* suffered various mental illnesses and physical ailments afterward. Others were supposedly fused to the ship's deck or completely vaporized and were never seen again.

## MOODUS NOISES

The Moodus Noises are thunderlike sounds that emanate from caves near East Haddam, Connecticut, where the Salmon and Moodus Rivers meet. The name itself is derived from the Native American word *machemoodus*, which means "place of noises." When European settlers filtered into the area in the late 1600s, the Wangunk tribe warned them about the odd, supernatural sounds. In 1979, seismologists showed that the noises were always accompanied by small earthquakes spread over a small area. But this doesn't explain the fact that no known fault line exists at Moodus. Nor does it describe how small tremors can generate big, bellowing booms. The mystery and the booms continue.

## ROCK CONCERT

Visitors to Pennsylvania's Ringing Rocks Park often show up toting hammers. Seems odd, but they're necessary for the proper tone. Ringing Rocks is a seven-acre boulder field that runs about ten feet deep. For unknown reasons, some of these rocks ring like bells when struck lightly by a hammer or other object. Because igneous diabase rocks don't usually do this, the boulder field has caused quite a stir through the years. In 1890, Dr. J. J. Ott assembled rocks of different pitches, enlisted the aid of a brass band, and held his own "rock concert."

## CRY ME A RED RIVER

A Mother Mary statue cries "tears of blood" at the Vietnamese Catholic Martyrs Church in Sacramento. It began crying in November 2005 when parishioners discovered a dark reddish substance flowing from her left eye. A priest wiped it away only to see it miraculously reappear a moment later. News of the incident spread quickly. Skeptics say that black paint used as eyeliner on the statue is the true culprit and that her "tears" are closer to this color than red.

# MEDICAL ODDITIES AT THE MÜTTER MUSEUM

Located at the College of Physicians of Philadelphia, the Mütter Museum is home to the world's most extensive collection of medical marvels, anatomical oddities, and biological enigmas.

Among the items on display the Mütter Museum are the conjoined livers of the world-famous Siamese twins, Chang and Eng; a selection of 139 Central and Eastern European skulls from the collection of world-renowned anatomist Joseph Hyrtl; and the preserved body of the "Soap Lady." Also on display are an assortment of objects that have been extracted from people's throats; a bevy of brains, bones, and gallstones; and a cancerous growth that was removed from President Grover Cleveland. There are also pathological models molded in plaster, wax, papier-mâché, and plastic; memorabilia contributed by famous scientists and physicians, plus a medley of medical illustrations, photographs, prints, and portraits.

Dr. Thomas Dent Mütter, a flamboyant and slightly fanatical physician obsessed with devising new and improved surgical techniques to cure diseases and deformities, donated the collection to the college in 1858. Mütter was ostracized by the medical community for both his methods and his predilection to preserve the remains of some of his more peculiar patients. The Mütter Museum officially opened its doors in 1863, and it has intrigued curious visitors ever since.

# CELEBRITY UFO SIGHTINGS

Reports of UFOs have been around since the pyramids or the Inca temples, both of which were allegedly constructed by visitors from outer space needing navigational aids. Judging from the following accounts, perhaps aliens are just doing a little celebrity watching.

**John Lennon**'s song "Nobody Told Me" touches on his experience with a UFO. In 1974, the former Beatle reported seeing a UFO outside his apartment in New York City. As he and a friend watched, the UFO drifted away, changing its shape with each rotation. Lennon took photos of the craft, but when he attempted to develop the film, it turned out blank. Lennon's friend called the police, who had received two other calls on the incident, and the *New York Daily News*, which had received five calls reporting a UFO on the East Side that night. *The New York Times* allegedly hung up on him.

Heavyweight boxing champ **Muhammad Ali** also claimed to have seen UFOs hovering over New York City. The occurrence was said to have taken place early in his career while he was working with his trainer, Angelo Dundee, in Central Park. Just before dawn, the two men observed a large, round UFO as it came out from behind the city skyline and moved slowly across the sky, a sighting that lasted about 15 minutes. Ali claimed multiple sightings. In one, he was a passenger in a car motoring along the New Jersey Turnpike when a cigar-shape craft hovered briefly over his vehicle.

**Ronald Reagan** is considered the first president to talk about the possibility of an alien invasion. He believed that if such a situation occurred, all the nations of the world should unite to fight off the attackers. Reagan even discussed this scenario with General Secretary Mikhail Gorbachev during their first summit meeting in Geneva in 1985.

Guitarist **Jimi Hendrix** often claimed to have been followed around by UFOs and frequently referred to them in his lyrics. In addition, Hendrix allegedly was saved from freezing to death in 1965 by an eight-foot-tall angel-like alien who thawed the snowdrift in which the musician's van was stuck. He also once told a *New York Times* reporter that he was actually from Mars.

During **Jimmy Carter**'s presidential election campaign of 1976, he told reporters that he once saw what could have been a UFO in 1969, before he was governor of Georgia. "It was the darndest thing I've ever seen," he said of the incident. He claimed that the object that he and a group of others had watched for ten minutes was as bright as the moon. Carter was often referred to as "the UFO president" after being elected because he filed a report on the matter.

# GHASTLY MEDIEVAL TORTURE DEVICES

## THE RACK

During medieval times, being interrogated meant experiencing excruciating pain as one's body was stretched on the infamous Rack. The operating premise was diabolically simple. Victims laid on their backs with arms extended while straps anchored the hands and feet to opposite ends of the table. The torture began when the operator rotated rollers at each end in opposing directions. At the very least, severe joint dislocations occurred. At worst, limbs were ripped clean off and death would result. Even when the tortured victim was subsequently released, they'd often be incapable of standing erect since muscle fibers stretched beyond a certain point lose their ability to contract.

## THE IRON MAIDEN

The Iron Maiden torture device differs wildly from the popular heavy metal band of the same name. Insidious in its intent, the sarcophagus-shaped instrument opened to allow the victim to step inside. Once there, protruding spikes on the front and back halves would spear the occupant as the door was closed. Agonies were prolonged because spikes were strategically positioned to find the eyes, chest, and back but not vital organs. As a result, death occurred only after the victim had bled out, an agonizing process that could last for days.

## THE PEAR

Despite sharing its name with a sweet fruit, there was nothing at all sweet about the Pear. Designed to be inserted in the most sensitive of the body's orifices (i.e., mouth, rectum, vagina), the pear-shaped torture tool was used as a punishment for those who had committed sexual sins or blasphemy. Once put in place, a screw mechanism caused pointed outer leaves to expand ever wider, resulting in severe internal mutilation.

## THE TONGUE-TEARER

Self-explanatory in name, the Tongue-Tearer worked precisely as advertised. Resembling a wire cutter with an eyebolt passing through its end grips, a victim's mouth was forced open as the Tongue-Tearer was employed. After finding purchase on its slippery quarry, the eyebolt at the opposite end of the device was tightened ever so slowly, until the tongue became completely detached from the horrified victim's mouth.

## THE LEAD SPRINKLER

With its innocuous sounding name, one might expect to find this item gracing a formal garden, not doing the devil's handiwork in a dank dungeon. Shaped like a maraca, the Lead Sprinkler held molten lead inside a perforated spherical head. The torturer would simply hold the device over the victim and give it a shake. The ensuing screams were the only music to come from this instrument.

# QUIRKY COLLECTIONS

## NAVEL FLUFF

In 1984, Graham Barker of Perth, Australia, started collecting his navel lint. Since then, he has seldom missed a day's "harvest" and collects an average of 3.03 milligrams each day; he currently has about 2½ jars of lint. He was rewarded for his efforts in 2000 when *Guinness World Records* declared his navel lint collection the world's largest.

## TRAFFIC SIGNS AND SIGNALS

Stephen Salcedo asks visitors to his Web site to refrain from calling the cops on him—all 500-plus traffic signs and signals in his collection were obtained legally. Salcedo started his collection in 1986 at age five. The Fort Wayne, Indiana, collector has always been attracted to the graphic design aspect of road signs and has a special fondness for older ones (pre-1960). The "treasure" of his collection is the street sign that stood on the corner near his childhood home in Merrillville, Indiana.

## POLICE AND PRISON RESTRAINTS

If the handcuff-collecting world has a celebrity, it is Stan Willis of Cincinnati. Since 1969, Willis has been collecting police and prison restraints and has built his reputation selling rare cuffs to other collectors. In 2003, *Guinness World Records* recognized his collection as the largest—it now contains nearly 1,400 items. He also collects police and fire department-related items.

## MUSTARD

Barry Levenson began his mustard collection in October 1986, with 12 jars he bought to soothe his grief when the Boston Red Sox lost to the New York Mets in the World Series. He vowed to assemble the largest collection of prepared mustard in the world. In April 1992, he opened the Mount Horeb Mustard Museum in Mount Horeb, Wisconsin. He now displays nearly 5,000 mustards from all 50 states and more than 60 countries, as well as historic mustard memorabilia.

## BARF BAGS

Although Steve Silberberg of Massachusetts has never been out of the United States, his 2,000-plus barf bags come from around the world. Silberberg began collecting "happy sacks"—as they're known in piloting circles—in 1981 and now has a wide range of bus, car, train, and helicopter bags as well. Although not the largest collection in the world (he guesses it might be the tenth largest), he does have the largest collection of non-transportation bags, including novelty bags not intended for use, as well as political and movie sickness bags. The treasures of his collection include those given away on the Disneyland Star Tours ride and one from the Space Shuttle.

# GHOST SHIP AHOY!

*Pirates of the Caribbean* movies have renewed interest in such folkloric figures as Davy Jones and The Flying Dutchman while simultaneously muddling their stories. At no time was Davy Jones captain of the famed ghost ship.

## DAVY JONES

"Davy Jones's Locker" is an old seafaring term for the bottom of the ocean, the grave of all those who perish at sea. There are numerous tales about the origin of the expression, most of which attempt to identify a real Davy Jones. One version has Jones running a pub in London, where he press-ganged unwary customers into serving aboard pirate ships by drugging them and then storing them in the pub's ale cellar or locker. Other stories relate Jones to Jonah, the biblical figure who spent three days and nights trapped in the belly of a big fish.

## THE FLYING DUTCHMAN

This term is often used to refer to a ghost ship that is doomed to sail the oceans forever, but it is more accurately a reference to the captain of the ghost ship.

Legend holds that in 1680, Dutch captain Hendrik Van der Decken's ship was wrecked in a terrible storm off the Cape of Good Hope at the southern tip of Africa. As the ship sank, the captain's dying words were a vow to successfully round the infamous Cape even if it took him until doomsday.

Over the years, whenever there is stormy weather off the Cape, seafarers have reported seeing a phantom ship battling the waves, with a ghostly captain at the wheel. In 1939, dozens of bathers on a South African beach reported sighting a 17th-century merchant vessel off the coast and then seeing it suddenly vanish into thin air.

# STRANGE AND UNUSUAL TALENTS

## RUBBERBOY: DANIEL BROWNING SMITH

Nicknamed "Rubberboy," Daniel is unique, even among his peers. Most contortionists are either forward benders or backward benders, but rarely both. Daniel, who is able to contort and dislocate his 5'8" body into almost any formation, is that rare exception, so much so that he holds three *Guinness World Records*. Daniel's opening and closing acts are especially awe-inspiring—he emerges from a tiny 19.5" x 13.5" x 16" box to begin and manages to fold himself back into the box before being carried off stage at the finale.

## THE AYALA SISTERS

When Michelle, Andrea, and Alexis Ayala enter the circus ring, the petite sisters juggle fire, twirl, and spin—all while hanging by their long locks. Traditional hair suspension acts go up and down more than the stock market, never leaving the performer suspended for more than a half minute. But the Ayala sisters, like their mother before them, remain aloft for nearly six minutes, only coming back to the circus floor long enough to gain momentum for their final dizzying, high-speed spin.

## THE WOLF BOY

Take one look at Danny Gomez and you'll realize there's something different about him. Born with a condition called hypertrichosis, his entire body, including his face, is covered with thick black hair. But Danny is about much more than his unusual physical appearance. He's been performing since he was a small child—more than 20 years—and his amazing skills include juggling, trampoline, trapeze, and even daredevil motorcycle stunts. Danny's warm personality and quirky sense of humor make him a favorite with audiences, especially children.

## TIM "ZAMORA THE TORTURE KING" CRIDLAND

Audience members may cringe while watching Zamora perform, but they never forget him. Using martial arts techniques combined with Eastern teaching, hypnosis, and an extensive knowledge of anatomy, Zamora astounds and shocks his fans with feats of mind over matter—jumping on and eating glass, sword swallowing, electrocution, and body skewering—only to emerge intact and unscathed. That can't always be said for the more squeamish members of the crowd.

## GEORGE "THE GIANT" MCARTHUR

At 7'3", George McArthur stands out among performers, but not just because of his imposing size. This multitalented gentle giant holds a *Guinness World Record* for having the most weight—1,387 pounds from slabs of cement—broken on his body while lying on a bed of nails. George started in the circus business as a fire-eater, a skill he learned while determined to rid himself of a fear of flames. Since then he's added sword swallowing, walking on broken glass, and straightjacket escapes to his performing repertoire.

# UNEXPLAINED MYSTERIES OF THE UNIVERSE

## BERMUDA TRIANGLE

This area in the Atlantic Ocean between Bermuda, Miami, and San Juan is legendary as the site from which an astoundingly high number of ships, small boats, and airplanes have allegedly disappeared. Although the United States Coast Guard does not officially recognize the Bermuda Triangle or maintain any data on the area, conspiracy theorists have spent countless hours documenting the mysteries of the region. Some researchers estimate that more than 2,000 boats and 125 planes have been lost there, including the famous Flight 19, and five Navy bombers that disappeared in 1945, followed by their search-and-rescue seaplane. Explanations for the disappearances include extraterrestrials that captured the boats and planes, deep-water earthquakes that caused freak waves, and time warps that took vessels to a different time or dimension.

## AREA 51

Officially, Area 51 is a remote strip of land about 90 miles north of Las Vegas that the Air Force uses to test new military aircraft. Unofficially, it's a storage and examination site for crashed alien spaceships, a meeting spot for extraterrestrials, a breeding ground for weather control and time travel technology, and possibly the home of a one-world political group. Because the U.S. government won't discuss what goes on at Area 51, inquiring minds have had to develop their own theories. In 1989, Bob Lazar, a former government scientist, told a Las Vegas TV station

that he worked on alien technology at a facility near
Area 51. Millions believed Lazar's story and Area 51's
mysterious reputation was sealed.

## NOSTRADAMUS

Whether you believe his predictions or not, 16th-century
French philosopher Nostradamus was an impressive guy.
After all, how many authors' books are still in print 450 years
after their first editions? *Les Prophéties*, first published in
1555, is a series of poems that predict major world events
in a vague, timeless manner that leaves much room for
interpretation. Nostradamus's followers credit him with
predicting the rise of both Napoleon and Hitler, the French
Revolution, the Great Fire of London, both World Wars, the
death of Princess Diana, the Apollo moon landings, and the
terrorist attacks of September 11, 2001, among other things.
Skeptics say the links between his prophecies and world
events are the result of misinterpretations or mistranslations,
or are so vague that they are laughable.

## STONEHENGE

Situated near Amesbury, England, Stonehenge is a
collection of giant stones standing in a circular formation.
Archaeologists estimate that the stones were erected
between 3000 and 1600 B.C. in three separate phases.
Visitors to the site have been hypothesizing as to its
origins for centuries, but various academics have credited
the Danes, the druids, the Romans, the Greeks, and the
Egyptians, among others. Just as many theories exist
regarding its purpose: a predictor of solar phenomena,
a means of communicating with heaven, a pre-historic
computer, a sacred place of worship, and more. Some

people even believe it's an extraterrestrial landing site and claim to have seen UFOs in the area.

## CROP CIRCLES

Art exhibit, practical joke, or universal mystery, crop circles have been captivating observers for decades. They occur when crops are flattened to form geometric patterns most visible from the sky. Crop circles are usually found in England but have also been spotted in Australia, South Africa, China, Russia, and other countries. In 1991, two men admitted they had created a number of the crop circles identified in England since 1978 by marking out circles with a length of rope and flattening the crops with iron bars and wooden planks. But "croppies," a group of scientists and paranormal enthusiasts, argue that some of the designs are far too complex for humans to create with simple tools. Croppies believe that some of the circles are the result of flying saucers that land in fields, freak wind vortexes, or ball lightning.

## Who Were Henry VIII's Tower of London Victims?

- Queen Catherine Howard, Henry's fifth wife, was beheaded for adultery on the Tower Green. With her went her lovers, Thomas Culpepper and Francis Dereham, and her lady-in-waiting, Jane Rochford.

- Jane Rochford was instrumental in the downfall of two queens: She testified against her husband, George Boleyn, and sister-in-law, Queen Anne, helping them to their graves by accusing them of incest; and she arranged trysts for Catherine Howard, a crime for which both women were executed.

- Desperate to marry Jane Seymour, Henry had his second queen, Anne Boleyn, executed on trumped-up charges of adultery and witchcraft. Accused and killed with Anne were her brother George, as well as Henry Norris, Francis Weston, and William Brereton, who had been close friends with the king. Anne's musician, Mark Smeaton, was also executed for supposed adultery with the queen.

- The royal House of Plantagenet nearly became extinct under Henry's rule. The Plantagenets were descended from earlier kings of England, primarily the profligate Edward III, and possibly had a better claim to the throne than the Tudors. Those who made this assertion publicly were often executed on petty or unfounded charges.

- Edward Stafford, Third Duke of Buckingham, was beheaded for being the leader of nobles who were openly resentful of King Henry VIII's reliance on lowborn ministers such as Cardinal Wolsey, the son of a butcher. Many historians believe Stafford was also killed because he was part of the royal Plantagenet family and had bragged that his family was more royal than Henry's.

- King Henry's paranoia grew as he edged closer to death, and Henry Howard, Earl of Surrey and son of the Duke of Norfolk, was one of those who paid the price. The king became convinced that the two noblemen were planning to grab the throne from Henry's son Edward when he died, so both were sent to the Tower. Henry Howard was beheaded, but his father, Thomas Howard, Third Duke of Norfolk, narrowly avoided losing his head when Henry VIII died the day before he was to be executed.

- Margaret Pole, the 67-year-old Countess of Salisbury, suffered one of the most gruesome beheadings on record. She refused to put her head on the block, saying that she was no traitor, and therefore had to be forced down. The executioner's first blow struck her shoulder. According to some accounts, she then jumped up and ran from the executioner, who struck her 11 times before she finally died.

- The longest-serving prisoner of the Tudor reign was Sir William de la Pole, who sat in the Tower of London for 37 years. Henry VII arrested Sir William for suspicion of treason because he was a Plantagenet and he and his brother were Yorkist heirs, the leading contenders for the English throne. Sir William was executed in 1513.

- Being Henry's most trusted minister provided no protection from the executioner. Thomas Cromwell rose to power in 1532 and was a major figure in the English Reformation. Like many of Henry's advisors, his fall was caused by his support for one of Henry's wives—in this case, his arrangement of the king's marriage to Anne of Cleves, whom Henry despised. Cromwell was sent to the block in 1540.

- Anne Askew was convicted as a heretic and executed for her Protestant beliefs. She had been arrested for preaching Protestant views and was cruelly racked to get the names of other prominent reformists. Queen Katherine Parr was nearly arrested after pleading for mercy for Anne, but her plea was rejected and Anne burned at the stake.

# 7 FAMOUS PEOPLE WHO DIED IN THE BATHROOM

**1. ELVIS PRESLEY:** The King of Rock 'n' Roll was born in Tupelo, Mississippi, on January 8, 1935. He was discovered in Memphis by Sun Records founder Sam Phillips, who was looking for a white singer with an African American sound and style. Elvis catapulted to fame following three appearances on *The Ed Sullivan Show* in 1956 and 1957. Although he was pushed off the charts by the British invasion in the early 1960s, he still sold more than a billion records in his lifetime. His movie career kept him in the public eye until his comeback album in 1968, and in the 1970s, he sold out shows in Las Vegas as an overweight caricature of his former self.

Elvis's addiction to prescription drugs was well known, and on August 16, 1977, he was found dead on the bathroom floor in his Graceland mansion. A vomit stain on the carpet showed that he had become sick while seated on the toilet and had stumbled to the spot where he died. A medical examiner listed the cause of death as cardiac arrhythmia caused by ingesting a large number of drugs.

**2. LENNY BRUCE:** Controversial comedian Lenny Bruce was born Leonard Alfred Schneider in October 1925. Bruce was famous in the 1950s and 1960s for his satirical routines about social themes of the day, including politics, religion, race, abortion, and drugs. His use of profanity—rarely done at that time—got him arrested numerous times. On August 3, 1966, Bruce, a known drug addict, was found dead in the bathroom of his Hollywood Hills home with a syringe, a burned bottle cap, and other drug paraphernalia. The official cause of death was acute morphine poisoning caused by an accidental overdose.

**3. ELAGABALUS:** Scandalous 3rd-century Roman emperor Elagabalus married and divorced five women, including a Vestal Virgin (a holy priestess), who under Roman law should have been buried alive for losing her virginity. Elagabalus also may have been bisexual. Objecting to his sexual behavior and his habit of forcing others to follow his religious customs, his grandmother Julia Maesa and aunt Julia Avita Mamaea murdered Elagabalus and his mother (Julia Maesa's own daughter) in the emperor's latrine. Their bodies were dragged through the streets of Rome and thrown into the Tiber River.

**4. ROBERT PASTORELLI:** Born in 1954, actor and former boxer Robert Pastorelli was best known as Candace Bergen's housepainter on the late '80s sitcom *Murphy Brown.* He had numerous minor roles on television and also appeared in *Dances with Wolves*, *Sister Act 2*, and *Michael*, as well as a number of made-for-TV movies. Pastorelli struggled with drug use and in 2004 was found dead on the floor of his bathroom of a suspected heroin overdose.

**5. ORVILLE REDENBACHER:** Orville Redenbacher, founder of the popcorn company that bears his name, was born in 1907, in Brazil, Indiana. Millions came to know him through his folksy television commercials for the specialty popcorn he invented. He sold the company to Hunt-Wesson Foods in 1976, but remained as a spokesperson until September 20, 1995, when he was found dead in a whirlpool bathtub in his condominium, having drowned after suffering a heart attack.

**6. ALBERT DEKKER:** Actor Albert Dekker, who appeared in *Kiss Me Deadly*, *The Killers*, and *Suddenly, Last Summer*, was blacklisted in Hollywood for several years for criticizing anti-communist Senator Joe McCarthy. Dekker later made a comeback, but in May 1968, he was found strangled to death in the bathroom of his Hollywood home. He was naked, bound hand and foot, with a hypodermic needle sticking out of each arm and obscenities written all over his body. The official cause of death was eventually ruled to be accidental asphyxiation.

**7. JIM MORRISON:** Born on December 8, 1943, Jim Morrison was best known as the lead singer for

The Doors, a top rock band in the late 1960s. His sultry looks, suggestive lyrics, and onstage antics brought him fame, but drug and alcohol abuse ended his brief life. On July 3, 1971, Morrison was found dead in his bathtub in Paris. He reportedly had dried blood around his mouth and nose and bruising on his chest, suggesting a massive hemorrhage brought on by tuberculosis. The official report listed the cause of death as heart failure, but no autopsy was performed because there was no sign of foul play.

# THE ROYAL DIRT

Queens, kings, and mistresses—in the backstabbing world of royal courts, people got into all sorts of crazy things.

- Edward III's notorious mistress, Alice Perrers, is said to have stolen the rings off the king's fingers as he died.

- Elizabeth I lost a fortune in gold and jewel decorations that came loose and fell off her clothes as she went about her daily business. This was a common problem for nobles at the time, and attendants were often charged with watching for fallen ornaments and discretely retrieving them.

- Jane Seymour, third wife of Henry VIII, picked out her wedding dress on the day her predecessor, Anne Boleyn, was executed.

- King Louis XV's longtime mistress, Madame de Pompadour, wielded so much power over the king she was known as "the real Queen of France."

- King Henry IV of England was a childhood friend of King Richard II, whom he later deposed.

- "Divorced, beheaded, died; divorced, beheaded, survived" is a popular rhyme to remember the fates of Henry VIII's six wives.

- Edward III was the first English king to claim the French throne. His claim was through his mother, Queen Isabella, and had been included as part of her marriage contract to Edward II. The French king's refusal to honor the contract was the spark that started the Hundred Years' War.

- Egyptian pharaohs often married their siblings because it was believed that pharaohs were gods on Earth and thus could marry only other gods.

- Queen Cleopatra of Egypt was the first ruler in 300 years who actually spoke Egyptian. The Ptolemaic pharaohs were Greeks descended from Ptolemy, one of Alexander the Great's generals, so Greek was the dominant language of their court.

- Richard II was so upset over the death of his first wife, Anne of Bohemia, that he had the house she died in destroyed.

- Emperor Augustus attempted to reform what he considered loose Roman morals. In a bit of irony, he then had to banish his daughter Julia for committing adultery.

# THE IDA B. WELLS STORY

Almost a century before Rosa Parks made her stand, activist Ida B. Wells made a similar point on a train in Tennessee.

Little known today, Ida B. Wells should certainly be included among the most famous Americans. She was born in 1862 to slave parents who were freed along with the rest of the slaves in 1865. When Wells was 16, her parents and youngest sibling died during a yellow fever epidemic. In order to keep her family together, Wells showed her budding strength as she took a job as a schoolteacher and raised her younger siblings.

Wells moved her family to Memphis, Tennessee; it was here that she experienced the act of racism that launched her career. Wells had bought a first-class train ticket for a "ladies'" car, but the conductor told her to move to the "colored" car to make room for a white man. When Wells refused, the conductor attempted to forcibly move her. As Wells later explained, "the moment he caught hold of my arm I fastened my teeth in the back of his hand." It took two more men to drag her off the conductor and off the train.

## LASHING OUT AGAINST LYNCHING

Wells sued the railroad company; she won the case in lower courts but lost the case in appeals in Tennessee's Supreme Court. The case served to instigate the fight for equality.

Wells became the co-owner and editor of *Free Speech*, an anti-segregationist newspaper in Memphis, and focused her energies on revealing the horrors of lynching. In her landmark book, *A Red Record: Tabulated Statistics and Alleged Cause of Lynching in the United States*, she showed how horrifyingly common the practice of lynching was, picking apart one popular excuse used to justify it: A black man's rape of a white woman. "Somebody must show that the Afro-American race is more sinned against than sinning," Wells said.

Wells argued that whenever the rape defense was brought into a lynching case, the truth was that it usually was a voluntary act between a white woman and a black man. Wells traced the history of this rape defense, and pointed out that white slave owners would often leave for months at a time, leaving their wives under the care of their black male slaves. In fact, she argued, white-black sexual liaisons were typically the other way around, with white owners sleeping with or raping female slaves.

Wells was the first scholar of note to unearth the hypocrisy behind the white man's so-called protection of white women's honor through lynching: "To justify their own barbarism," Wells wrote, "they assume a chivalry they do not possess...no one who reads the record, as it is written in the faces of the million mulattoes in the South, will for a minute conceive that the southern white man had a very chivalrous regard for the honor due the women of his own race." Wells concluded that the brutal lynching epidemic was really the result of fear for economic competition, combined with white men's anger at voluntary liaisons between white women and black men, along with racism.

## CONTINUING THE FIGHT

Wells's work continued until her death in 1931. She married fellow activist and writer F. L. Barnett in 1895. Together the couple had four children and worked to help African Americans in Chicago. Wells also was a founding member of the NAACP and the first president of The Negro Fellowship League. In 1930, shortly before her death, she ran for the Illinois Senate.

# Whatever Happened to Van Gogh's Ear?

Great artists are people of almost unfathomable passion. And with a recognized genius like Vincent Van Gogh, you'd expect the sort of passion that rises to another level entirely. Throw said genius into a love triangle with friend and roommate Paul Gauguin and a trollop named Rachel, and you just know that someone's not going to make it out in one piece. In this instance, it was Van Gogh who came out on the losing end.

For Van Gogh, lopping off his own left earlobe has the distinction of being the artist's ultimate act of mental instability—even overshadowing his suicide. His self-mutilation has brought him unprecedented (if posthumous) attention. Most know the ear anecdote; some know that he did it for a woman. What has been lost to history is the final resting place of that little chunk of genius—whatever happened to the ear?

In December 1888, following an argument with Gauguin,

who was also an artist, Van Gogh came at his friend with an open razor. Gauguin held him off. The content of the argument is likewise lost in the shadows of history; Van Gogh had been drinking absinthe almost nonstop, and he was prone to fits of violence and depression.

Back in his room, Van Gogh sliced off the lower portion of his left ear. He wrapped his severed lobe in a piece of cloth and walked to one of the many brothels he was known to frequent. Upon arrival, he requested a prostitute named Rachel. (Rumor has it that Van Gogh and Gauguin were in competition for this working girl's affections.) When she appeared at the door, he handed her what is easily one of the worst gifts of all time: a bloody piece of ear flesh. Rachel fainted dead away. Feeling dejected, Van Gogh slumped back to his room and passed out. When discovered by Gauguin and others, Van Gough exhibited only faint signs of life and was taken to a hospital.

This is where the ear passes out of the story. The artist checked himself in and out of a mental institution before taking his own life seven months later. Presumably, based on her, shall we say, unenthusiastic response to her beau's unique gift, Rachel discarded the ear upon returning to her senses. Since the only mention of Rachel in the history books is in the paragraph describing Van Gogh's short visit (the books do not even make mention of her last name), what she actually did with the ear remains a mystery.

Such is the sad fate of the artist: putting such painstaking effort into a project, only to have the final product go unappreciated.

# HISTORY'S MADDEST RULERS

## VLAD THE IMPALER

Everyone has heard of the infamous Count Dracula. Half man, half bat, this beastly hybrid lived to drink human blood. But not everyone knows that novelist Bram Stoker's inspiration for the evil madman came from an actual person who was much worse than he's been portrayed. Vlad III Dracula (1431–1476) governed Wallachia, a Hungarian principality that later merged with neighbors Transylvania and Moldavia to form Romania. To say that Dracula ruled with an iron fist barely scratches the surface—an "iron stake" is more accurate. During his six-year reign of terror, it is believed that Dracula murdered as many as 40,000 people whom he considered enemies. Most of these unfortunates met their end by impalement, hence Dracula's ominous moniker. With a sharpened stake as wide as a man's arm, his victims were often pierced from the anus to the mouth. The madman often blinded, strangled, decapitated, hanged, boiled, burned, or skinned his victims. Once, a concubine hoping to spare her life claimed that she was carrying Dracula's child. When he discovered she was lying, he had her womb cut open and remarked, "Let the world see where I have been."

## IDI AMIN DADA

To the eye, Ugandan president Idi Amin Dada (1925–2003) was a deceptive contradiction. Viewed as a cartoonlike character by the press (*Time* dubbed him a "killer and clown, big-hearted buffoon and strutting martinet"), the former major general nevertheless found a way to kill an estimated 300,000 people while in power. Many of his victims were killed to squelch the ruler's paranoid fears of being overthrown. Others were eliminated simply for his own ghoulish pleasure. Known as the "butcher of Uganda," Amin reportedly kept severed heads in his refrigerator and may have eaten some of his victims. And allegedly, when Amin learned that his second wife was pregnant with another man's child, he had her dismembered. After the atrocity, he ordered her remains stitched together so he could show her corpse to their children.

## JUSTIN II

In the final days of his reign, Byzantine Emperor Justin II (c. 520–578) descended into an overwhelming insanity that was only briefly punctuated by moments of lucidity. Accounts tell of a daft ruler who went mad after a nervous breakdown. Monitored closely by attendants, the emperor sometimes needed to be restrained to keep him from committing undue harm upon himself or others. The crazed ruler would often lunge at his attendants in an attempt to bite them, and reports suggest that he actually devoured a number of his faithful servants during his reign.

## KING GEORGE III

Great Britain's King George III (1738–1820) suffered recurring bouts of dementia during his reign. Believed to be suffering the ill effects of porphyria, a blood disorder that can produce psychotic symptoms, the king often acted in an outlandish manner. Fits of gloom and melancholy often alternated with excited periods where the king would talk incessantly and act strangely. During one such bout, George III reportedly spoke nonsense for a period lasting some 58 hours. But whether or not the king was insane, his "caregivers" were a bit suspect as well, at least by today's standards. Doctors often tried bleeding him to remove bad substances. When this failed, another doctor decided to draw the poison out of his brain by cutting small holes in his forehead. The king was also confined to a straightjacket, denied heat in the winter, and fed chemical agents that did nothing more than make him vomit.

## VITELLIUS

If an unquenchable bloodlust is the hallmark of a true madman, Roman emperor Aulus Vitellius Germanicus Augustus (A.D. 15–69) ranks near the top. Simply known as Vitellius, he took perverse joy in watching his victims squirm. His actions sound like something lifted from a Stephen King novel, yet they are reportedly true. Consider this: On impulse, and purely for his own amusement, Vitellius would summon personal friends and acquaintances to his court, then order them killed, or do the deed himself. On one occasion, two sons begging for their father's life were executed beside him. At another time, Vitellius gave a glass of poisoned water to a thirsty man stricken with fever and watched in utter glee as it took effect. Psychological tortures also factored heavily into this madman's repertoire. The ruler once issued a reprieve to a subject who was to be executed. As the man praised the emperor for his mercy, Vitellius ordered him killed in his presence saying that he wished to "feast [on] his eyes." His motives for such loathing are shrouded in mystery, but in the end, Vitellius was tortured, killed, and thrown in the Tigris River by the leader of an opposing faction.

## CALIGULA

The famed Caligula (Gaius Caesar Augustus Germanicus) (A.D. 12–41) served as emperor of Rome from A.D. 37 until his death. During that time, he reputedly engaged in long-term incestuous trysts with his sisters; forced losers of an oratory competition to erase their wax tablets with their tongues; ordered men's heads shaved (due to his own insecurity over his baldness); bestowed a consulship and priesthood upon his favorite horse; and ordered spectators to fight lions and tigers to the death during a shortage of criminals. In A.D. 41, Caligula was stabbed to death by his own Praetorian guards. Live by the sword; die by the sword.

# WALT DISNEY: THE MAN BEHIND THE MOUSE

- As a youngster, Walt Disney made extra spending money by selling drawings to his neighbors.

- At age 16, Disney tried to join the military but was rejected for being too young. He joined the Red Cross instead. He was sent to France, where he drove an ambulance.

- Disney grew his trademark mustache at the age of 25.

- The first commercially released Mickey Mouse cartoon, *Steamboat Willie*, was also the first Disney cartoon to feature synchronized sound. It premiered in New York City on November 18, 1928.

- Disney provided the voices for both Mickey and Minnie Mouse for nearly 20 years.

- Disney's first animated feature film, *Snow White and the Seven Dwarfs*, cost nearly $1.5 million to produce.

It was a huge gamble for the Disney studio but went on to tremendous financial success and critical acclaim.

- Following the success of *Snow White*, Disney and his brother, Roy, gifted their parents with a new house close to their studios. A month later, their mother died from asphyxiation caused by a broken furnace in the new home. Disney never recovered from the tragedy.

- Disney won a total of 32 Academy Awards.

- Although television made him world-famous, Disney experienced terrible stage fright every time he had to step in front of the camera.

## Who Was Mona Lisa?

It's been one of history's great debates: Who posed for Leonardo da Vinci when he painted art's most famous face in the early 1500s? You would think the missing eyebrows would be a dead giveaway. How many eyebrow-less ladies could there have been wandering around Italy? As it turns out, quite a few—it was a popular look at the time.

The leading theory has always been that Lisa is Lisa Gherardini, the wife of wealthy Florentine silk merchant Francesco del Giocondo. A 16th-century historian, Giorgio Vasari, made this claim in *The Lives of the Artists*, noting that the untitled painting was often called "La Gioconda,"

which literally means "the happy woman" but can also be read as a play on the name Giocondo. (If you're wondering, "Mona" is simply a contraction of ma donna, or "my lady," in Italian; the title is the equivalent of "Madam Lisa" in English.)

Vasari was infamous for trusting word of mouth, so there's a possibility that he got it wrong. Therefore, historians proposed many alternative Lisas, including Leonardo da Vinci's mom, various Italian noblewomen, a fictitious ideal woman, and a prostitute. Some believed that da Vinci's painting was a disguised portrait of da Vinci himself, noting how his features in other self-portraits resemble Lisa's.

In 2005, a manuscript expert at Heidelberg University Library in Germany, Armin Schlecter, closed the case. Looking through one of the books in the library's collection—a very old copy of Cicero's letters—Schlecter discovered notes in the margin written in 1503 by Florentine city official Agostino Vespucci. Vespucci, who knew da Vinci, described some of the paintings that Leonardo was working on at the time. One of the notes mentions a portrait of Lisa del Giocondo, aka Lisa Gherardini, proving fairly conclusively that Vasari had the right Lisa.

Historians know a bit about Lisa's life. She was del Giocondo's third wife; she married him when she was 16 and he was 30, a year after his second wife had died. They lived in a big house, but it was in the city's red light district. She likely sat for the portrait soon after the birth of her third child, when she was about 24. She had five children altogether and died at age 63.

# PRESIDENTIAL PECULIARITIES

- When he was elected, America's first president **George Washington** (1789–1797) had only one tooth and wore dentures made from hippopotamus and elephant ivory.

- After a long feud, **John Adams** (1797–1801) and **Thomas Jefferson** (1801–1809) finally called a truce and developed a friendship that lasted the rest of their lives. Both men died on July 4, 1826—the 50th anniversary of the adoption of the Declaration of Independence.

- **James Madison** (1809–1817) was the smallest president, weighing 100 pounds and standing 5'4" tall.

- **William Henry Harrison** (1841) was the first president to die in office. During his lengthy inaugural speech, he contracted a cold that quickly developed into pneumonia.

- Two decades after leaving the White House, **John Tyler** (1841–1845) joined the Confederacy and became the only president named a sworn enemy of the United States.

- During his presidency, **Franklin Pierce** (1853–1857) allegedly ran over a woman with his horse. He was arrested, but the case was dropped due to lack of evidence.

- **Abraham Lincoln** (1861–1865) was the only president to receive a patent; it was for a device designed to lift boats over shoals.

- **Warren G. Harding** (1921–1923) suffered his first nervous breakdown at age 24 and spent time in a sanitarium run by J. H. Kellogg of breakfast cereal fame.

- The first Catholic president, **John F. Kennedy** (1961–1963) was also the first to have been a Boy Scout.

- **Richard M. Nixon** (1969–1974) wanted to be an FBI agent. He applied to the Bureau but wasn't accepted.

- At age 19, **George H. W. Bush** (1989–1993) became the youngest pilot in U.S. Navy history. He went on to fly 58 combat missions during World War II and was shot down in 1944 (he was rescued after four hours on a life raft).

# WOMEN YOU WOULDN'T WANT TO MESS WITH

### WU WHO?

Empress Wu, China's sole female leader, displayed a talent for ruthlessness and cruelty that belied her station as a member of the so-called "weaker sex." Born in A.D. 624, she became a fifth-level concubine to Emperor Taizong at age 14. Educated, beautiful, and gifted, she quickly caught the emperor's eye and earned the pet name "Charming Lady."

"Cunning lady" would have been more appropriate. Wu soon learned attention equaled power. Elevated to "second grade" concubine under Emperor Kao Tsung, Wu still wanted more. After securing the new emperor's favor by bearing him two sons, she devised a plan to eliminate her competition by strangling her own infant daughter and blaming the baby's death on the jealous actions of the empress and head concubine.

The emperor sided with Wu and elevated her to the throne. Empress Wu then ordered the "murderers" be executed, allegedly first having their hands and feet amputated and then having them drowned. That level of cruelty set the tone for the rest of her reign. When a stroke incapacitated the emperor, she took over his duties and dispatched any opposition by means of exile, murder, or forced suicide.

After her husband died, Wu installed her weakest son as emperor so that she could continue to rule through him. When he eventually proved difficult to manage, she facilitated his abdication and formally assumed the crown. But while Wu was inarguably brutal, she was also brilliant. The empress is credited with elevating the stature of women in Chinese society and with advancing agriculture and lowering taxes.

## BLOODY BATHORY

Though born into nobility in A.D. 1560, Erzsebet (aka Elizabeth) Bathory was anything but noble. Known as "Hungary's National Monster," she was a sadistic serial murderess who is rumored to have tortured and killed up to 650 women, aided by a motley crew consisting of her children's wet nurse, a dwarflike manservant, and a brawny servant woman rumored to be a witch.

Frankly, Bathory's cruelty sounds like the stuff of legend. She reportedly began torturing peasant girls for entertainment by lashing and bludgeoning them. She moved on to dragging the women naked through the snow, and then drenching them with water until they froze to death. After Bathory's husband died, she moved to their castle at Cachtice. There she befriended Anna Darvulia, a sadist like herself (and rumored to be her lover, as well).

The relationship with Darvulia emboldened Bathory to engage in even more atrocious behavior. Legend has it that one time when Bathory was too weak to partake in more vigorous torture activities, she had a servant girl delivered to her bedside so she could bite the flesh from her. Other rumors persist that Bathory bathed in the blood of virgins to maintain her skin's youthful appearance.

It's hard to point to an exact cause for her outlandish actions. Bathory's parents were cousins, part of Hungary's elite aristocracy. Some believe this inbreeding caused her madness; others attribute Bathory's heinous crimes to her volatile temperament and unrestrained sense of upper-class privilege.

Since Bathory's victims were peasants, the ruling class (who mainly consisted of Bathory's relatives) tended to turn a blind eye to her vicious pastimes. But things changed after Darvulia died in 1609. Bathory then met Erszi Mjorova, the widow of one of Bathory's tenant farmers. It was Mjorova who may have encouraged Bathory to refine her tastes toward more upper-class victims.

When it was discovered Bathory's appetite had changed to girls of noble birth, her cousin the King of Hungary ordered her arrest. Convicted of 80 counts of murder, Bathory's noble heritage protected her from the death penalty. Instead, she was sentenced to be walled up alive in her castle. Unrepentant to the end, she lived in such a state for four years, until she was discovered dead by a guard in 1614.

## LALAURIE THE GORY

Delphine LaLaurie is another woman who has inspired countless tales and ghost stories. The wife of a prominent New Orleans dentist (her third husband, whom she married in 1825), she led a dual life. Publicly she was a gracious hostess, well known for her lavish parties and charmingly flirtatious disposition. But to the servants at the family's mansion in the city's French Quarter, Madame LaLaurie was a brutal mistress capable of unspeakable evil.

LaLaurie's life was by all accounts privileged and perfect. Eventually, however, the malevolent side of her behavior surfaced publicly. One night, a neighbor reported seeing a young servant girl fall (some say jump) to her death from the top of LaLaurie's three-story home while being chased by her hostile mistress. As a reprimand, the authorities removed the house slaves and fined the couple $300. The servants were then auctioned off to the highest bidders—who, coincidentally, were LaLaurie's relatives. She repurchased the slaves and returned them to her service.

Things appeared to settle down at the LaLaurie home until a fire broke out in 1834. When firefighters arrived to put out the blaze, they discovered two slaves chained to the stove. Apparently, the servants had set fire to the kitchen on purpose to attract attention to the atrocities taking place inside the mansion.

This is where it gets ugly. Implored by the servants to look in the attic, the rescuers uncovered horrifying evidence of LaLaurie's evil. Although no one's entirely sure what was found, there are stories of horrifying experiments being done on the slaves. Some describe more than a dozen naked bodies, both dead and alive, chained to the walls or strapped to operating tables. One man had a hole cut in his head with a stick inserted to stir his brains. A caged woman had her arms and legs broken and reset to resemble a crab. Body parts were scattered everywhere.

Although Dr. LaLaurie is rumored to have known about his wife's grisly hobby, he was not thought to be a participant in her gruesome experiments. His wife, meanwhile, escaped the city before she could be brought to justice. However, a marker in Alley 4 of St. Louis Cemetery No. 1 indicates her body was returned to New Orleans from Paris for burial following her death in 1842.

# TALL TALES ABOUT NAPOLEON

Napoleon Bonaparte, one of the most successful and brutal military leaders of all time, had a short fuse and was often shortsighted. But he was not, as is popularly believed, short in stature.

## SLIGHTED BY HISTORY

It turns out that an error in arithmetic contributed to history's perception of Napoleon as a small man. The only known measurement of Bonaparte came from his autopsy, which reported a height of 5'2". But it was not taken into account that this measurement was calculated in French units. Translating to slightly more than 168 centimeters, his height was actually 5'6" by the English Imperial system. This was above average for a 19th-century Frenchman.

Another possible reason for this misconception is the fact that Napoleon kept himself surrounded by a group of relatively tall guardsmen. Napoleon was never seen in public without his "imperial guard." These soldiers averaged six feet in height and would have towered over Napoleon.

## A NAPOLEON COMPLEX

Napoleon wasn't short, but his temper was. Over time, the notion that the general's irascible, aggressive personality stemmed from his small size has been applied to any small-statured man who uses his temper to compensate for his height. This is referred to as a "Napoleon Complex," and though psychologists regard it as a negative social stereotype, it also proves to be a myth. In 2007, researchers at the University of Central Lancashire studied the effect of height on aggression in men. Using heart monitors to gauge reactions, scientists found that taller men were more likely to respond to provocation with aggressive behavior.

As Napoleon himself said, "History is the version of past events that people have decided to agree upon." It turns out that history cut Napoleon about four inches short.

# What Do They Do With Your Body If You Donate It to Science?

You can rest assured that scientists don't take donated cadavers out for wild parties or prop them in passenger seats just to use the carpool lanes. Typically, donating your body to science means willing it to a medical school, where it will be dissected to teach medical students about anatomy.

Fresh cadavers aren't as critical to medical schools as they once were, thanks to detailed models, computer simulations, and a better ability to preserve corpses. But they're still a much-appreciated learning aid. If you have a rare deformity or disease, your corpse will be especially useful.

Medical schools aren't allowed to buy bodies, rob graves, or go door-to-door recruiting volunteers, so they rely on potential donors initiating contact. If you want to donate your body, you'll need to find a medical school in your area with a body donation program. Your state's anatomical board is usually a good place to start. Once you've found a program, you fill out some legal paperwork and perhaps get a body donor identification card to carry in your wallet. Some schools will cover the cost of transporting your corpse to the school, within a certain distance, as well as cremation costs. Other schools won't pay for transportation.

This is very different from organ donation, which you can arrange in many states by adding a note to your driver's license and sharing your wishes with your family. If you're an organ donor and die under the right circumstances (you're brain-dead but on a respirator), the doctors may extract your heart, kidneys, lungs, liver, pancreas, or small intestine and whisk the pieces to the organ recipient. If you aren't on a respirator when you die, your organs won't be usable. Doctors can extract the organs, corneas, and skin tissue for transplant within 24 hours after death.

If you've already donated your organs, most medical schools won't accept what's left of your body. You're also out of luck if you died from a major trauma, had a contagious disease, or underwent major surgery within 30 days of your passing. Even when you're dead, it seems, getting into medical school is difficult.

# 8 MEDICAL MYTHS

**1. CHOCOLATE AND FRIED FOODS GIVE YOU ACNE:** Some speculate that this myth dates back to the baby boom generation, who had worse acne than their parents and also more access to chocolate and fried foods. Wherever this idea came from, it's wrong. Pimples form when oil glands under the skin produce too much of a waxy oil called sebum, which the body uses to keep skin lubricated. But when excess sebum and dead skin cells block pores, that area of the skin gets irritated, swollen, and turns red—the telltale signs of a pimple. It is unknown why sebaceous glands produce excess sebum, but hormones are the prime suspects, which explains why teenagers are affected more than others. Stress and heredity may also be factors, but chocolate bars and onion rings are off the hook.

**2. COFFEE WILL SOBER YOU UP:** If you've had too much to drink, no amount of coffee, soda, water, or anything else is going to sober you up. The only thing that will do the trick is time. The liver can metabolize only about one standard drink (12 ounces of beer, 6 ounces of wine, or 1.5 ounces of hard liquor) per hour, so if you're drinking more than that every 60 minutes, you'll have alcohol in your system for some time. The idea of coffee's sobering effect may have started because caffeine acts as a stimulant, counteracting the sedative effect of alcohol to a small degree. However, it has no effect on the amount of alcohol in the blood.

**3. COLD WEATHER CAN GIVE YOU A COLD:** "Put your jacket on or you'll catch a cold!" How times have you heard that? You may not want to tell her this, but dear old Mom was wrong. Viruses (more than 200 different kinds) cause colds, not cold weather. In order for you to catch a cold, the virus must travel from a sick person's body to yours. This usually happens via airborne droplets you inhale when an infected person coughs or sneezes. You can also get a cold virus by shaking hands with an infected person or by using something where the virus has found a temporary home, such as a phone or door handle. Colds are more prevalent during the colder months because people tend to spend more time inside, making it much easier for viruses to jump from person to person.

**4. CRACKING YOUR KNUCKLES CAUSES ARTHRITIS:** The knuckles are the joints between the fingers and hand, and these joints contain a lubricant called synovial fluid.

When you crack your knuckles, you are pulling apart two bones at the joint, which means the synovial fluid has to fill more space. This decreases the pressure of the fluid, and dissolved gases that are present, such as nitrogen, float out of the area in tiny bubbles. The bursting of these bubbles is the familiar sound we hear when someone "cracks" his or her knuckles. This bubble-bursting is not the same as arthritis, which is when the body's immune system attacks joints. However, constant knuckle-cracking can injure joints and weaken fingers.

**5. TOO MUCH SUGAR MAKES KIDS HYPERACTIVE:** Many parents limit sugary foods, thinking they cause hyperactivity. It's right to restrict these treats, but the reasoning is wrong. These high-calorie foods offer little nutrition and can lead to obesity and other problems, but no scientific evidence says sugar causes hyperactivity. Sugar can provide a short-term energy boost, but that isn't the same as hyperactivity. What about that unruly child in the grocery store throwing a fit with a sucker in his mouth and candy clutched in each fist? His parents probably haven't set appropriate behavior limits, and they most likely give him what he wants—which is more candy.

**6. SWALLOWED GUM TAKES SEVEN YEARS TO DIGEST:** Some misconceptions are hard to swallow, but people have been chewing on this one for years. This myth has probably been around since chewing gum became popular in the late 19th century and most likely originated thanks to a single word: indigestible. Gum is comprised of flavor, sweeteners, softeners, and gum base. The body is able to break down the first three ingredients, but gum base is indigestible. That simply means your body can't dissolve it and extract nutrients. In the end, gum base works its way through your digestive system much like fiber—in two or three days it goes out in basically the same shape it went in.

**7. WAIT 30 MINUTES AFTER EATING BEFORE SWIMMING:** For a kid, nothing ruins the fun of a carefree summer day like a worried parent banning swimming right after the big cookout, fearing that the child will get cramps and drown. There is a slight chance of minor abdominal cramping, but for the vast majority of people, this isn't dangerous. The body does divert blood flow from the muscles to the gastrointestinal system to spur digestion, but not in amounts that diminish muscle function. Listen to your body and swim when you're comfortable—just like you probably don't run a marathon right after Thanksgiving dinner, you don't want to start swimming laps right after a seven-course picnic. It is perfectly safe, though, to eat a light meal and then get wet. After all, athletes commonly eat right before competing.

**8. YOU CAN GET THE FLU FROM A FLU SHOT:** Vaccinations are misunderstood because they are created from the offending viruses themselves. But when you get a flu shot, you're not being injected with a whole virus—you're receiving an inactivated, or dead, virus. That means the part of the virus that can infect you and make you sick is turned off, but the part of the virus that stimulates your body to create antibodies is still on. The body's antibodies will kill the flu virus should you come into contact with it later. Even pregnant women are advised to get flu vaccinations, so you know they're safe. The only people who should avoid them are those who have severe allergies to eggs, because eggs are used to create the vaccines. No vaccine is 100 percent effective, so there is still a chance you can get the flu after receiving the shot, but that doesn't mean the vaccination gave it to you.

# Do Identical Twins Have Identical Fingerprints?

It would help many criminals if they did: Courtroom revelations of "mysterious long-lost twins" would probably skyrocket. But fortunately for law enforcement, everybody has distinct fingerprints, including two people with identical DNA.

Why? Because DNA doesn't completely dictate the way we develop. We are born the way we are because of a combination of genetics and random environmental factors in the womb. In the case of fingerprints, DNA roughly dictates how ridge patterns will be formed. In other words, genetics determines whether a fingerprint will be an arch, a whorl, a loop, or a mix of different varieties.

A variety of influences in the uterus, including how the skin contacts amniotic fluid and how the bones are grow during fingerprint formation, determine how the ridges end and split. These pattern alterations of the ridges, collectively known as minutiae, are what give you unique fingerprints. Interestingly, identical twins generally have a similar number of fingerprint minutiae and ridges, even though the patterns differ.

It's not just fingerprint patterns that grow differently. Random forces in the womb can give twins unique skin blemishes and even shape their faces differently. In fact, if one twin has a better connection to the placenta, he or she can eat better and might be significantly bigger at birth than his or her womb mate. Hey, it's never too early to get a step ahead in a sibling rivalry.

# BODY ODDITIES: UNUSUAL FACTS

- Don't stick out your tongue if you want to hide your identity. Similar to fingerprints, everyone also has a unique tongue print!

- Humans shed about 600,000 particles of skin every hour. That works out to about 1.5 pounds each year, so the average person will lose around 105 pounds of skin by age 70.

- An adult has fewer bones than a baby. We start off life with 350 bones, but because bones fuse together during growth, we end up with only 206 as adults.

- Did you know that you get a new stomach lining every three to four days? If you didn't, the strong acids your stomach uses to digest food would also digest your stomach.

- Your nose is not as sensitive as a dog's, but it can remember 50,000 different scents.

- The small intestine is about four times as long as the average adult is tall. If the small intestine weren't looped back and forth upon itself, its length of 18 to 23 feet wouldn't fit into the abdominal cavity, making things rather messy.

- The source of smelly feet, like smelly armpits, is sweat. And people sweat buckets from their feet. A pair of feet has 500,000 sweat glands and can produce more than a pint of sweat per day.

- The air from a human sneeze can travel at speeds of 100 miles per hour or more—another good reason to cover your nose and mouth when you sneeze!

- Blood has a long road to travel: Laid end to end, there are about 60,000 miles of blood vessels in the human body. And the hard-working heart pumps the equivalent of 2,000 gallons of blood through those vessels every day.

- You may not want to swim in your spit, but if you saved it all up, you could. In a lifetime, the average person produces about 25,000 quarts of saliva—enough to fill two swimming pools!

- Blondes may or may not have more fun, but they definitely have more hair. Hair color helps determine how dense the hair on your head is, and blondes (only natural ones, of course) top the list. The average human head has 100,000 hair follicles, each of which is capable of producing 20 individual hairs during a person's lifetime. Blondes average 146,000 follicles. People with black hair tend to have about 110,000 follicles, while those with brown hair are right on target with 100,000 follicles. Redheads have the least dense hair, averaging about 86,000 follicles.

- If you're clipping your fingernails more often than your toenails, that's only natural. The nails that get the most exposure and are used most frequently grow the fastest. Fingernails grow fastest on the hand that you write with and on the longest fingers. On average, nails grow about one-tenth of an inch each month.

- No wonder babies have such a hard time holding up their heads: The human head is one-quarter of our total length at birth but only one-eighth of our total length by the time we reach adulthood.

# What Did They Use for Birth Control in the Old Days?

Tough question. It's not information that got written down—at least not often. Some hints are found in the ancient writings of doctors and naturalists. They show that fruits and herbs played a big role in controlling fertility. An Egyptian scroll of medical advice that's 3,500 years old tells how to end a pregnancy at any point: Mix the unripe fruit of acacia with honey and other items to be soaked up by an absorbent pad of plant fiber; insert the pad into the vagina, and an abortion will follow. (Dissolved acacia produces lactic acid, which is a spermicide.)

Other old texts show that herbal birth control was brewed into teas. The leaves of pennyroyal (a type of mint) and parts of many plants that look like weeds to us could be brewed as a "morning-after" cure for unwanted pregnancies. Juniper berries, willow bark, mugwort, aloe, anise, dittany, and certain ferns were all used. Seeds from the plant Queen Anne's lace or from pomegranates were eaten for the same reason, as were figs. People in the Middle Ages and the Renaissance knew many of these plant-based solutions. In Shakespeare's *Hamlet*, Ophelia plays with the herb rue, a weed known to induce abortion. Rue is found throughout the Americas, too, and many native groups used it to end pregnancies.

What about condoms, sponges, and other devices? Illustrations thousands of years old show men using condoms, though the earliest condom found dates to 1640. It's made of sheep intestines. Goodyear began mass production of rubber condoms in 1843.

Female condoms, or cervical dams, have also been around for millennia. They've included seedpods, oiled paper, seaweed, lemon or pomegranate halves, beeswax, and even moss. History records the use of spermicidal potions made from oils, vinegar, rock salt, wine, and herbs.

Superstition and ignorance about the properties of certain ingredients played roles in some of these birth-control methods. Modern research on animals shows that some of these ingredients would have resulted in lower pregnancy rates or increased instances of miscarriage. However, some of these substances also are toxic, which would have made the birth-control benefits moot.

# 28 PHOBIAS AND THEIR DEFINITIONS

1. Ablutophobia—fear of washing or bathing
2. Acrophobia—fear of heights
3. Agoraphobia—fear of open spaces, crowds, or leaving a safe place
4. Ailurophobia—fear of cats
5. Alektorophobia—fear of chickens
6. Anthropophobia—fear of people
7. Anuptaphobia—fear of staying single
8. Arachnophobia—fear of spiders
9. Atychiphobia—fear of failure
10. Autophobia—fear of oneself or of being alone
11. Aviophobia—fear of flying
12. Caligynephobia—fear of beautiful women
13. Coulrophobia—fear of clowns
14. Cynophobia—fear of dogs
15. Gamophobia—fear of marriage
16. Ichthyophobia—fear of fish
17. Melanophobia—fear of the color black
18. Mysophobia—fear of germs or dirt
19. Nyctophobia—fear of the dark or of night
20. Ophidiophobia/Herpetophobia—fear of snakes
21. Ornithophobia—fear of birds
22. Phasmophobia/Spectrophobia—fear of ghosts
23. Philophobia—fear of being in love
24. Photophobia—fear of light
25. Pupaphobia—fear of puppets
26. Pyrophobia—fear of fire
27. Thanatophobia/Thantophobia—fear of death or dying
28. Xanthophobia—fear of the color yellow

# How Many Diapers Does a Baby Go Through Before Being Potty-Trained?

The average newborn runs through (no pun intended) about 12 to 16 diapers per day, according to Diapering Decisions, a supplier of cloth diapers. If we define a newborn as being two weeks old or younger, a baby goes through 168 to 224 diapers in just the first fourteen days of life.

Luckily, the pace slows a bit after that. Between three and six months of age, you'll change a baby 10 to 12 times a day; between six and nine months, 10 times a day; from nine months to the end of the first year, 8 times a day; and up to eighteen months, count on 6 to 8 changes a day.

When it will end depends on your kid. It might be as early as two years; it might take as long as four. WebMD.com says that the average for boys is 38 months; for girls, the average is 36 months. Thus, you'll change little Georgie between 8,008 and 10,150 times before he's ready to tackle the potty. You'll change little Susan between 7,672 and 9,702 times.

## ALL OF YOUR GRAY MATTER MATTERS

If you think about it—using your whole brain, of course—the theory that humans use only 10 percent of their brains is 100 percent wrong. The persistent and widespread misconception falls apart when logic is applied. As it turns out, we need all of our gray matter. Here's why:

- The brain is not made of muscle, despite what many people think. But if it were, and we used only 10 percent of it, it would quickly degenerate. The adage "Use it or lose it" applies to muscle. The unused 90 percent of the brain would shrink to nothingness.

- What about brain cancer and gunshot wounds to the head? Victims would have a 90 percent chance that the tumor or bullet would lodge in the useless part of the brain. If only that were true.

- An organ that requires so much energy to maintain would not have evolved if it were mostly useless. The brain consumes 20 percent of the body's oxygen and glucose. The time and energy required to develop the brain is responsible for the vulnerability of human infants and the remarkable length and difficulty of human pregnancy and childbirth.

- If seeing is believing, look no further than PET, CAT, or MRI scans of the brain. All reveal there is activity throughout the brain, even during sleep.

## FORMULATING A FALSEHOOD

The 10 percent myth began with some confusing information exchanged among scientists, and it gained traction with the false claims of advertisers, psychics, and questionable "healers."

Throughout the 1800s, it was understood that different parts of the brain were responsible for different functions. Scientists just weren't sure which part matched which function—and that's still partially true today. The idea that different parts perform discrete activities makes the idea of a "functionless" brain area inconceivable.

In the early 1900s, scientists used electricity to zap small parts of the brain to observe what it made people do (e.g., scream, blink, or lift an arm). The subjects appeared to do nothing when certain areas of the brain were zapped. These parts, called the "silent cortex," were considered by some to be functionless. They are now known to be responsible for language and abstract thought.

Others pointed to the rare cases of lobotomy patients who appeared to act normally. Of course, no one had anywhere near 90 percent of their brain lobotomized, and lobotomy patients who functioned "normally" were usually those who had been operated on as children. Young brains, we now know, are able to rewire neural pathways to compensate for damage.

## PERPETUATING THE SAME FALSEHOOD
In the first half of the 20th century, scientists made vague claims about unused parts of the brain. Psychics, mystics, cultists, and various religious leaders took this up as evidence that their particular creed was the conduit to the brain's untapped powers. The 10 percent claim became popular somewhere around mid-century in advertisements for healing centers and self-help lectures. The myth is still popular in promotional ads for everything from airline companies to TV series.

# How Long Can You Live Without Sleep?

Nobody knows for certain, but Dr. Nathaniel Kleitman, the father of modern sleep research, said: "No one ever died of insomnia." Still, what doesn't kill you can still have some nasty side effects.

Various studies have revealed that missing just one night of sleep can lead to memory loss and decreased activity in certain parts of the brain. So if you're planning an all-night cram session for the eve the big mid-term, you may be better off closing the book and getting a good night's sleep.

Then again, maybe not. Each person's body and brain handle sleep deprivation differently. Some folks are all but useless after one night without shuteye, while others function normally. It's largely a matter of biology.

Take Tony Wright. In May 2007, the 43-year-old British gardener kept himself awake for 226 hours. He said that he was aiming for the world's sleeplessness record and wanted to prove that sleep deprivation does not diminish a person's coherence. Wright admitted to some odd sensory effects during his marathon without sleep, but he insisted his mental faculties were not compromised.

Wright's quest didn't amount to much more than a lot of lost sleep. *Guinness World Records* stopped acknowledging feats of insomnia in 1990 after consulting with experts at the British Association for Counseling and Psychotherapy. The experts believe that sleep deprivation threatens psychological and physical well-being. Muscle spasms, reduced reaction times, loss of motivation, hallucinations, and paranoia can all be triggered by sleep deprivation.

# 19 STRANGE ILLNESSES AND DISORDERS THAT ALMOST NOBODY GETS

**1. PROGERIA:** It might seem like you're getting old fast, but for people who suffer from progeria—a disease for which there were only 80 certified cases worldwide as of 2011—premature aging is a reality. This condition, which speeds up the aging process, causes people to grow old and die within just a few years.

**2. FOREIGN ACCENT SYNDROME:** People afflicted with FAS wake up one day suddenly speaking with a completely different accent—often from countries they've never even been to. Doctors think the odd disorder is caused by brain injury, though they aren't sure exactly what kind.

**3. HARLEQUIN ICHTHYOSIS:** Children with this extremely rare disorder are born with thick, scaly patches of skin covering their face, like a suit of armor. Unfortunately, the armor harms more than protects, and most afflicted with harlequin ichthyosis die in childhood.

**4. KURU:** Kuru is a rare neuromuscular disease, but you probably don't need to worry about catching it—unless you're a cannibal. That's because the disease is only transmitted by eating infected human brain tissue. The only known cases of Kuru occurred among the Fore tribes—people of New Guinea who practiced cannibalistic funeral rites until the 1950s.

**5. PANTOTHENATE KINASE-ASSOCIATED NEURODEGENERATION:** PKAN is a rare degenerative brain disease that causes spasms, tremors, loss of speech, and blindness. It commonly strikes children before the age of 10, making it both terrifying and heartbreaking. Luckily, doctors estimate that only one in a million individuals are affected.

**6. SLEEPING BEAUTY SYNDROME:** For people suffering from Sleeping Beauty syndrome—more officially known as Kleine-Levin syndrome—it's no fairy tale. Sufferers of this rare hypersomniac condition go through long stretches of their life sleeping. Worse, when they're awake they're spaced out and nonfunctional.

**7. MERMAID SYNDROME:** Officially known as sirenomelia, this condition is a birth defect in which an infant is born with its legs fused together. The syndrome only strikes about one in 100,000 births, and to date only one child born with the disease has been known to survive longer than 10 years.

**8. COLD URTICARIA:** Nobody likes cold weather, but imagine being allergic to it. People suffering from cold urticaria develop rashes and hives when exposed to cold weather.

**9. HYPERTHYMESIC SYNDROME:** People with hyperthymesic syndrome never forget what day their anniversary falls on—

or anything else, for that matter. People suffering from this extremely rare disorder remember every detail of every day for most of their lives.

**10. REDUPLICATIVE PARAMNESIA:** People with this unusual and rare mental disorder believe that they are in a place different from where they actually are. For example, mental patients with this disorder often believe the room they are in is their house or that the hospital is in another part of the country.

**11. CAPGRAS SYNDROME:** This rare psychological disorder makes sufferers suspicious of their loved ones or even their own reflections.

**12. FREGOLI DELUSION:** People with Fregoli delusion have the opposite problem of those with Capgras syndrome—they believe someone is following them and that everybody they see is that person dressed up in disguise.

**13. FIELDS CONDITION:** This degenerative neuromuscular condition is so rare that there are only two known cases in the history of recorded medical science—identical twins Catherine and Kirstie Fields.

**14. COTARD DELUSION:** People suffering from the little-seen mental disorder take low self-esteem to its limits. At the extreme, patients believe they do not exist. Others believe that organs are putrefying, limbs have vanished, or blood is disappearing from the body.

**15. LANDAU KLEFFNER SYNDROME:** In this rare childhood neurological disorder, children suddenly lose the ability to comprehend and express language. Even more strangely, sufferers of this condition sometimes completely regain speech within a few years.

**16. CRANIOPAGUS PARASITICUS:** One of the rarest of all conditions, craniopagus parasiticus describes a birth defect in which a "parasitic" twin head is attached to a newborn's head. Only 10 cases of this condition have been reported in the history of medical literature.

**17. SUBJECTIVE-DOUBLE SYNDROME:** Don't tell a person suffering from subjective-double syndrome that you saw somebody who looked like him or her on the street. He or she already believes that they have one or more doppelgängers.

**18. DANCING EYES–DANCING FEET SYNDROME:** Dancing eyes–dancing feet syndrome isn't nearly as fun as it sounds. Symptoms of this obscure condition include irregular, rapidly twitching eyes and random muscle spasms that make sitting and standing nearly impossible.

**19. ALIEN HAND SYNDROME:** This unusual condition is pretty much what it sounds like—the sensation that a force completely beyond your control is manipulating your hands.

# Can You Cry Underwater?

Human weeping comes courtesy of something called the "lacrimal apparatus," a deceptively complex system—

including glands, canals, and ducts—that produces tears. The tears themselves are complex, too. Although they taste like saltwater, tears actually contain an important enzyme called lysozyme, which has the pretty sweet ability to dissolve bacteria on contact. Though we most often think of tears as the product of sadness, your lacrimal apparatus is constantly hard at work producing tears for the cleansing and moistening of your eyes, providing its tear-delivery system 24 hours a day.

Which brings us back to the question: Can you cry underwater? It is certainly biologically possible to do so—just as it is possible to sweat underwater and to urinate underwater. The production of tears from the lacrimal glands does not stop merely because of the presence of water. One can imagine, however, that if you swim down deep enough without adequate protection, the increased water pressure could have adverse effects on the lacrimal apparatus. (Of course, at that point, your ability to cry would be the least of your concerns.)

If on the other hand we define crying in the more colloquial sense—as in the wailing, gasping sobs of tots at the public pool—it seems highly unlikely that crying underwater would last more than a millisecond before one drowned. So the next time you find yourself heartbroken at the public pool, save your weeping and wailing for when you are above water.

# HOW TO SURVIVE A SINKING CAR

Thousands of drivers accidentally steer themselves into lakes or rivers every year. Most cars take only a few minutes to submerge—would you know how to get out alive? If you know how to handle the situation, the disaster doesn't have to turn deadly.

## • Stay calm and unbuckle

The first rule of thumb is never panic. Remain calm, unfasten your seatbelt, and get ready to exit the vehicle.

## • Roll down the window

Don't wait: Roll down your driver-side window as quickly as you can. Even electric windows will open if you try soon enough. If it doesn't work, you'll have to smash the glass. A heavy object is your best bet, but you can try to kick out the window with your feet, too. (Take an easy precaution and leave a screwdriver or hammer inside your glove box, just in case.) Aim for the bottom or corner edge of the window. Whatever you do, don't try to open the door—there's too much pressure from the water outside.

## • Work your way out

Take a deep breath and force yourself out through the open space. Then start swimming upward.

## • If the window won't open

If you can't get the window open or broken, your only option is to wait until your car has almost been overtaken with water. Climb into the back seat, as it'll be the last to fill up. Unlock the door right away so you don't forget. Then, once the water is as high as your neck, push the door open— once the water is inside the car, there should be enough pressure for the door to give without much trouble. As soon as it opens, swim as fast as you can out of the vehicle and toward the surface.

# THE ALL-TIME
## DEADLIEST DISASTERS

### DINO-B-GONE

The deadliest disaster in Earth's history may have struck long before humans even existed. According to leading scientific theory, the dinosaurs (and many others) checked out when a massive asteroid slammed into Earth about 65 million years ago. The resulting destruction dwarfs anything that's happened since.

- Scientists estimate the asteroid was about six miles wide—bigger than Mount Everest.

- The energy of the impact was likely equal to hundreds of millions of megatons. That's about a million times more powerful than the explosion you would get if you detonated all the nuclear bombs in the world at once.

- The asteroid hit in what is now the Gulf of Mexico,

blasting massive amounts of scorching steam and molten rock into the sky and creating tsunamis that were hundreds of yards high and that moved 600 miles per hour.

- The resulting shock wave rocked the entire planet and killed everything for hundreds of miles around.

- Molten rock fell back to Earth for thousands of miles around the impact, setting much of the planet on fire.

- The kicked-up material darkened the atmosphere everywhere and generated nitric acid rain.

- All told, the asteroid wiped out as much as 75 percent of all life on the planet.

## KING OF PLAGUES

The worst disaster on record in terms of human death toll was the Black Death—a pandemic thought to be bubonic plague, pneumonic plague, and septicemic plague, all caused by bacteria carried by fleas.

- The plague infected the lymphatic system, resulting in high fever, vomiting, enlarged glands, and—in the case of pneumonic plague—coughing up bloody phlegm.

- Bubonic plague was fatal in 30–75 percent of cases; pneumonic plague was fatal in 75 percent of cases; and septicemic plague was always fatal.

- Between 1347 and 1350, the plague spread across Europe and killed approximately 75 million people—nearly half the European population.

- Improvements in sanitation helped bring the Black Death to an end, but the plague still pops up now and then in isolated outbreaks.

## AN EXTRA LARGE SHAKE
The deadliest earthquake and string of aftershocks in recorded history rocked Egypt, Syria, and the surrounding areas in 1201.

- Of course, nobody was measuring such things back then, but experts believe the initial quake ranked as a magnitude 9.

- As luck would have it, Egypt was already experiencing a major drought, and damage from the quake exacerbated the problem, leading to mass starvation (and a bit of cannibalism to boot).

- Historians put the total death toll at about 1.1 million.

## THE STORM OF SEVERAL CENTURIES
The deadliest storm on record was the Bhola Cyclone, which hit East Pakistan (now Bangladesh) on November 13, 1970.

- The storm's winds were in excess of 120 miles per hour when it finally hit land.

- It generated an astonishing storm surge of 12 to 20 feet, which flooded densely populated coastal areas.

- Parts of the Ganges River actually turned red with blood.

- According to official records, 500,000 people died (mainly due to drowning). Some sources put the total at closer to a million.

## BLAST FROM THE PAST

The deadliest known volcanic eruption occurred in Indonesia in 1815.

- When the 13,000-foot Mount Tambora erupted, it blew two million tons of debris 28 miles into the air and continued to burn for three months.

- The seismic energy generated massive tsunamis, leading to widespread flooding.

- Three feet of ash covered much of the surrounding area, killing all vegetation and resulting in a devastating famine.

- The debris in the atmosphere darkened skies all around the world, creating "The Year Without a Summer," and continued to block sunlight for years afterward.

- In 1816, parts of the United States saw snow in June and July, thanks to the persistent cold caused by the eruption on the other side of the world.

- All told, the eruption claimed more than 70,000 lives.

# NEW STRAITSVILLE'S UNDERGROUND FIRE

A labor strike started a fire underground, where it had enough fuel to burn unabated—for more than 125 years.

In 1884, miners striking against the Plummer Hill Mine in the town of New Straitsville, Ohio, crammed oil-soaked timbers into bank cars, set them on fire, and rolled them deep into the mine. By the time company executives discovered the fire, it had grown too large to extinguish. As the months passed, owners estimated that Hocking Valley mines had lost $50 million in damages due to the fire that refused to go out. This fire continues to burn like a massive coal stove more than 100 years later, and it still has plenty of fuel. In Perry County village, locals have literally fried eggs over hot cracks in the ground.

The state doesn't consider the fire dangerous so long as it is monitored, but area residents say they can feel the heat and sometimes see parts of fields and yards collapse from it. They claim the fire goes dormant, only to inexplicably reignite itself again and again.

In the early to mid-1900s, entrepreneurs started hot-spot tours and brewed coffee over the hot cracks. Signs identified the spots as "Devil's Garden," "Inferno Land," and "Hell's Half Acre." Famed journalist Ernie Pyle, a roving reporter in the 1930s, came to New Straitsville to feel the fire. "Just to look around over these rolling green hills of southern Ohio," he wrote, "you wouldn't believe that hell is only a few feet underneath."

Before World War II, federal employees tried to contain the fire by constructing rock barriers and trenches, but the blaze outwitted them. The fire had calmed down by 1940. These days, few tourists stop to ask to fry an egg over a crack in the ground, although local residents insist it can still be done, with help from the fire that refuses to burn out.

# 7 DESTRUCTIVE EARTHQUAKES

Every year, earthquakes cause thousands of deaths, either directly or due to the resulting tsunamis, landslides, fires, and famines. Scientists have measured the strength of tremors on the Richter scale, which assigns magnitude in numbers, like 6.0 or 7.2. A 5.0 tremor is equivalent to a 32-kiloton blast, nearly the explosive power of the atomic bomb dropped on Nagasaki in 1945. Here are some destructive earthquakes in recent history.

## 1. MISSOURI: DECEMBER 16, 1811

The New Madrid fault—near where Missouri, Kentucky, Arkansas, and Tennessee meet—witnessed an 8.0 or greater magnitude quake more than 200 years ago. The shaking spread so far that church bells reportedly rang in Boston, more than 1,500 miles away! It had dramatic effects on the area's geography, lifting up land enough to make the Mississippi River appear to flow upstream. Fortunately, the sparsely populated area suffered only one death and minimal property damage.

## 2. SAN FRANCISCO: APRIL 18, 1906

The Great San Francisco Earthquake—a 7.8 magnitude tremor—brought down structures across the Bay Area. In San Francisco, buildings crumbled, water mains broke, and streetcar tracks twisted into metal waves. But the majority of the 3,000 deaths and $524 million in property damage came from the massive post-tremor fire, which spread rapidly across the city in the absence of water to quell the flames. People as far away as southern Oregon and western Nevada felt the shaking, which lasted nearly a minute.

## 3. SOUTHERN CHILE: MAY 22, 1960

The strongest earthquake ever recorded—9.5 on the Richter scale—was actually a succession of large quakes that struck southern Chile over the span of a few hours. A catastrophic tsunami ensued, severely ravaging the Chilean coast before rushing across the Pacific to pulverize Hawaii. In Chile, landslides, flooding, and the eruption of the Puyehue volcano less than two days later followed the quake. All told, there were more than 5,700 deaths and $675 million in property damage in Chile, as well as Alaska, Hawaii, Japan, and the Philippines.

## 4. ALASKA: MARCH 28, 1964

The most powerful tremor in U.S. history—lasting three minutes and measuring 9.2 on the Richter scale—struck Prince William Sound in Alaska. Only 15 people died in the quake itself, but the resulting tsunami, which reached more than 200 feet high at Valdez inlet, killed 110 more people and caused $311 million in property damage.

## 5. PERU: MAY 31, 1970

A 7.9 magnitude quake just off the western coast of South America caused more than $500 million in damage and killed 66,000 Peruvians, with building collapses responsible for most of the deaths.

## 6. CHINA: JULY 27, 1976

This quake, a 7.5 on the Richter scale, was one of many major tremors over the years along the "Ring of Fire," a belt of heavy seismic activity around the Pacific Ocean. It struck Tangshan, then a city of one million people near China's northeastern coast. Official Chinese figures indicate around 250,000 deaths, but other estimates are as high as 655,000.

## 7. INDONESIA: DECEMBER 26, 2004

This massive earthquake just off the west coast of the island of Sumatra, and the tsunami that followed, killed at least 230,000 (and perhaps as many as 290,000) people in 12 countries—including about 168,000 in Indonesia alone. It registered 9.1 on the Richter scale and will long be remembered for the devastating waves that brought fatalities to countries all around the Indian Ocean. Scientists say the tremor was so strong that it wobbled Earth's rotation on its axis by almost an inch.

# HIGH TIDE: TALES OF SURVIVAL

Humankind has been subjected to every imaginable hostile condition, but very little beats the grueling stories of survival for days, weeks—even months—lost at sea.

## HOLD ON TIGHT

Ocean-going tales of survival have a certain mythic status. They bring to mind epic travels and age-old yarns of sea monsters and mermaids. Yet legend aside, even factually verified survival stories seem implausible. To be stranded on the sea (and to live to tell the tale) seems, well, unreal.

A hierarchy applies when gauging the relative extremity of a sea survival story. Those in cold water are the worst off, since hypothermia sets in within minutes. Survival time also depends on whether the person is holding onto something or treading water. Survival time is also cut short by solitude—humans have a difficult time being alone for extended periods. The best-case scenario, if one exists, is to be stranded on a boat, in warm water, along with some comrades. What follows are some record breakers that run the gauntlet of these hapless scenarios.

## JUAN JESUS CAAMANO:
## SURVIVED 13 HOURS WITH NO BOAT IN COLD WATERS

In 2001, a fishing boat capsized off the coast of Spain. Nine of the 16 men made it into a lifeboat; another two jumped into the frigid waters without bodysuits (and died immediately), while five others got their suits on before the boat sank.

Two of those five were 36-year-old Juan Jesus Caamano and his brother-in-law. Their boat had sent out a mayday signal before sinking, so planes, helicopters, and ships from several countries were sent to look for the victims. After only four hours, the nine men in the lifeboat were saved. Experts, who estimated a man in Caamano's circumstances could survive a maximum of 3½ hours, were surprised when, after 13 hours, Caamano was found alive, afloat in the stormy waters, tied to his dead brother-in-law. In all, six men died.

## LAURA ISABEL ARRIOLA DE GUITY:
## SURVIVED SIX DAYS; FOUND CLINGING TO
## DRIFTWOOD IN WARM WATERS

In 1998, Hurricane Mitch ravished Central and Latin America, killing more than 7,000 people in Honduras alone. Isabella Arriola, 32, lived in a small coastal Honduran village that was literally swept away by the ocean. She survived for six days with no life jacket, drifting in and out of consciousness, while clinging to driftwood. She survived high waves and winds that climbed to 185 miles per hour.

Arriola was eventually spotted by a coastguard aircraft and was rescued by helicopter. Unfortunately, her husband, children, and half her village had perished in the storm.

## STEVEN CALLAHAN:
## SURVIVED 76 DAYS ON A SMALL RAFT

In 1982, Steven Callahan, a naval architect, was participating in a sailing race when his boat was damaged during a storm and sank in the Atlantic Ocean. Callahan managed to salvage a tiny amount of food before setting off in an inflatable rubber raft. He survived for 76 days on rainwater, fish, and seabirds before being rescued by a fishing boat. Callahan's extensive background and experience with the high seas helped him survive the ordeal. He holds the longest known record for surviving alone on a raft.

## MARALYN AND MAURICE BAILEY:
## SURVIVED 117 DAYS ON A SMALL RAFT

In 1973, British couple Maralyn and Maurice Bailey set out on an ambitious voyage from England to New Zealand on their yacht, which was struck by a large whale and capsized off the coast of Guatemala. Maurice happened to be an expert on maritime survival skills; before they boarded their rubber raft, they collected a small amount of food, a compass, a map, an oil burner, water containers, and glue. When the Baileys ran out of food, they caught sea animals with safety pins fashioned into hooks. After two months, the raft started to disintegrate, and it needed constant care. Finally, after 117 days, a small Korean fishing boat rescued them.

# STRANGE CATASTROPHES

## THE LONDON BEER FLOOD

In 1814, a vat of beer erupted in a London brewery. Within minutes, the explosion had split open several other vats, and more than 320,000 gallons of beer flooded the streets of a nearby slum. People rushed to save as much of the beer as they could, collecting it in pots, cans, and cups. Others scooped the beer up in their hands and drank it as quickly as they could. Nine people died in the flood—eight from drowning and one from alcohol poisoning.

## THE GREAT SIBERIAN EXPLOSION

Around 7:00 A.M. on June 30, 1908, a mysterious 15-megaton explosion flattened 60 million trees in remote Siberia. The huge blast, which occurred about five miles above the surface of Earth, traveled around the world twice and triggered a strong, four-hour magnetic storm. Magnetic storms occur about once every hundred years, and can create radiation similar to a nuclear explosion. These storms start in space and are typically accompanied by solar flares.

The 1908 explosion may have started with a comet of ice, which melted and exploded as it entered Earth's atmosphere. Or, it may have been an unusual airburst from an asteroid. Others believe that the source was a nuclear-powered spacecraft from another planet. However, no physical evidence of the cause has ever been found.

## THE BOSTON MOLASSES DISASTER

On an unusually warm January day in 1919, a molasses tank burst near downtown Boston, sending more than two million gallons of the sticky sweetener flowing through the city's North End at an estimated 35 miles per hour. The force of the molasses wave was so intense that it lifted a train off its tracks and crushed several buildings in its path. When the flood finally came to a halt, molasses was two to three feet deep in the streets, 21 people and several horses had died, and more than 150 people were injured. Nearly 100 years later, people in Boston can still smell molasses during sultry summer days.

## OREGON'S EXPLODING WHALE

When an eight-ton sperm whale beaches itself in your town, what do you do? That's a question residents of Florence, Oregon, faced in November 1970. After consulting with the U.S. Navy, town officials decided to blow up the carcass with a half ton of dynamite. Spectators and news crews gathered to watch but were horrified when they were engulfed in a sandy, reddish mist and slapped by flying pieces of whale blubber. A quarter mile away, a car was crushed when a gigantic chunk of whale flesh landed on it. No one was seriously hurt in the incident, but when the air cleared, most of the whale was still on the beach. The highway department hauled the rest of it away.

# Can People Get Sucked Out of Planes?

Unfortunately, yes. All sorts of objects, including human beings, can be hurled out of shattered windows, broken doors, and other holes in the skin of an aircraft. The problem in any case like this is explosive decompression—a situation in which the keys to survival include the height at which the plane is flying and the size of the aircraft cabin itself.

Most passenger planes are pressurized to approximate an altitude of 8,000 feet or less. If there is a break in the skin of the plane at an altitude considerably higher than that—commercial jets normally fly at 30,000 feet or more—all sorts of bad things can happen. And quickly. For one thing, a lack of oxygen will render most people unconscious in little more than a minute at 35,000 feet.

As for being sucked out of the plane, this sort of tragedy generally occurs when the decompression is very sudden. The difference in pressure between the inside and outside of the plane causes objects to be pulled toward the opening. Whether or not someone survives sudden decompression depends on several things, including luck.

Critical care nurse Chris Fogg was almost sucked out of a medical evacuation plane on a flight from Twin Falls, Idaho, to Seattle in 2007. Fogg had not yet buckled his seat belt when a window exploded while the plane was flying at approximately 20,000 feet. His head and right arm were pulled out of the window, but Fogg held himself inside the aircraft with his left hand on the ceiling and his knees jammed against a wall.

Fogg, who weighed 220 pounds, summoned enough strength to push himself backward, which allowed air to flow between his chest and the window. This broke the seal that had wedged him in the opening. The pilot managed to get the plane to a lower altitude, and everyone aboard—including a patient who had been hooked to an oxygen device—survived the ordeal.

Not everyone has been so fortunate in cases of explosive decompression. In 1989, a lower cargo door on a United Airlines flight came loose at 23,000 feet, and the loss of pressure tore a hole in the cabin. Nine passengers were sucked out of the plane, along with their seats and the carpeting around them. A year earlier, an 18-foot portion of roof tore off an Aloha Airlines flight at 24,000 feet, hurling a flight attendant out into the sky.

Although scenes of people and debris whistling all over the place in adventure movies have been exaggerated, the threat of explosive decompression is real—even if it is rare. It's a good idea to take the crew's advice about wearing your seat belt at all times, and if there is a sudden loss of oxygen, put on that mask in a hurry. They're not kidding about the possible consequences.

# 11 PEOPLE WHO FELL FROM A GREAT HEIGHT AND SURVIVED

**1.** In 1960, a boating accident sent seven-year-old Roger Woodward over Niagara Falls (Horseshoe Falls, specifically). Wearing only a bathing suit and a life preserver, he plummeted 161 feet, missed the rocks at the foot of the falls, and emerged unscathed. For 43 years, he was the only person to survive the drop without protective gear.

**2. (and 3.)** In 1979, newlyweds Kenneth and Donna Burke fell from a sixth-story balcony while posing for pictures during their wedding reception. They landed on grass 72 feet below, narrowly missing a concrete patio and brick wall.

**4.** In 2004, a 102-year-old Italian woman toppled over the railing of her fourth-story balcony. A plastic playhouse broke her fall, and apart from an arm fracture, she was fine.

**5.** In 1999, Joan Murray from Charlotte, North Carolina, couldn't get her parachute to open after jumping from a plane at 14,500 feet (2.7 miles). At 700 feet, her reserve chute opened, but then quickly deflated. She hit the ground at 80 miles per hour, landing directly on a mound of fire ants. Doctors believed the shock of more than 200 ant bites actually kept her heart beating. Less than two years later, she went on her 37th skydive.

**6. (and 7.)** When a man in Kuala Lumpur, Malaysia, returned home and caught two burglars in his apartment, they jumped out the window—16 stories up—and landed in a dumpster. The trash cushioned their fall.

**8.** John Kevin Hines is one of about two dozen people to survive leaping off the Golden Gate Bridge in San Francisco. He jumped in 2000, when he was 19 and suffering from severe depression. He immediately regretted his decision and turned himself around during the 25-story drop so he could hit feet first, like a diver. He hit the water at about 75 miles per hour, breaking his back and cracking several vertebrae. After he recovered, he launched a speaking campaign calling for the addition of protective barriers on the bridge.

**9.** In 2007, brothers Alcides and Edgar Moreno were washing the windows on a New York high-rise when the cables holding their support swing failed. Edgar hit a fence below and died instantly. Alcides survived the 47-story fall by holding on to the 16-foot swing. Physicists believe the aluminum platform acted like a giant surfboard, slowed by air currents rising between the buildings.

**10.** In 1985, mountain climber Joe Simpson broke his leg while he and Simon Yates were descending Siula Grande in Peru. Yates and Simpson tied their ropes together, and Yates steadily lowered Simpson down the mountain. But when Simpson slipped off a cliff, Yates cut the rope to keep from falling himself. Yates assumed Simpson was dead and made his way back to camp. After falling 100 feet into a crevasse, Simpson dragged himself back to base camp. He made the six-mile trek in three days, with no food or water.

**11.** Serbian flight attendant Vesna Vulovic was the only survivor when Yugoslav Airlines Flight 367 broke up over Czechoslovakia in 1972. An explosion, apparently from a bomb, ripped the DC-9 plane apart when it was 33,333 feet (6.3 miles) in the air. When the wreckage fell to the ground, a villager found Vulovic lying in a piece of fuselage. She made a full recovery, and in 1985 was inducted into *Guinness World Records* for surviving the highest fall without a parachute.

# Can You Outrun Lava?

It depends on how fast you can run and how fast the lava flows. The absolute fastest humans in the world can run a little faster than ten meters per second, but only for 100 meters. For a 5,000-meter Olympic race, peak human performance is just more than six meters per second. Assuming you'll have a major adrenaline boost due to the dire circumstances, we'll say that you can maintain a speed of three to five meters per second. This speed could vary greatly, however, depending on your physical condition and the distance you need to run, which might be several kilometers.

The speed of lava is affected by its temperature and viscosity (which are related), the angle of the slope it is flowing, and the expulsion rate of the volcano. There are different types of volcanoes and varieties of lava. Some, you could probably outwalk; other types of lava would swallow and incinerate an Olympic-class runner before he or she took a single step.

A pyroclastic flow isn't actually made of lava—it's a column of hot ash and gas that collapses under its own weight and roars down the side of the volcano like an avalanche. These flows can reach speeds of 40 meters per second—you have no chance of outrunning them.

Basaltic lava has a high temperature and low viscosity, which means that it can move quickly, approaching speeds of 30 meters per second. However, many basaltic flows are much slower—two meters per second or less. You could outpace it for a while, but basaltic lava is relentless and often flows ten or more kilometers from the volcano before cooling and coming to a stop. You might outrun the slower flows, but it would be a challenge.

Mount Kilauea in Hawaii has been continuously issuing basaltic lava flows since 1983. Occasionally, the flows extend to nearby towns, most of which have been abandoned. When there are Hawaiians in the path of the lava, however, they are able to run away from the generally slow flows.

Rhyolitic lava moves very slowly because it has a relatively low temperature and high viscosity. It may move only a few meters in an hour. It is still dangerously hot, however, so while you can easily outpace it with a brisk walk, you shouldn't dilly-dally.

# THREE-RING TRAGEDIES: CIRCUS DISASTERS

For more than 200 years, various circuses have brought smiles to the faces of American children of all ages. They're popular attractions, but they've also been the scene of horrendous disasters. Here are five of the most memorable.

## THE WALLACE BROTHERS CIRCUS TRAIN DISASTER

On August 6, 1903, two trains owned by the Wallace Brothers Shows were involved in a calamitous rear-end collision at the Grand Trunk Railroad Yard in Durand, Michigan. Twenty-three people were killed instantly, and several others died shortly after; nearly 100 individuals were injured. Numerous animals also perished in the crash, including three camels, an Arabian horse, a Great Dane, and an elephant named Maud. The *Owosso Argus Press* described the aftermath this way: "The scene that followed is indescribable, the cries and groans from the injured persons and frightened passengers, the roars from the terrified animals and the escaping steam aroused the whole city, and hundreds rushed to the scene to assist in every way in the sad task of caring for the dead and wounded."

## THE HAGENBECK-WALLACE CIRCUS TRAIN DISASTER

In the early morning hours of June 22, 1918, the Hagenbeck-Wallace Circus train was struck by an empty troop train just outside Hammond, Indiana. Of the 300 passengers asleep in the circus train, 86 were killed and more than 127 were injured. As a result of the ensuing fire, fed by the wood-constructed Pullman cars, many of the dead were burned beyond recognition. Thanks to assistance from its competitors who loaned equipment and performers, the Hagenbeck-Wallace Circus had to cancel only two performances.

## THE HARTFORD CIRCUS FIRE

Perhaps the nation's best-known circus disaster is the devastating fire that broke out during an afternoon performance of the Ringling Brothers and Barnum & Bailey Circus on July 6, 1944, in Hartford, Connecticut. An estimated 167 people—most of them children—died in the blaze and the ensuing mayhem, and several hundred were injured (exact totals vary depending on the source). The cause of the fire remains a mystery, but investigators blame the speed with which the fire spread on the fact that the massive circus tent had been waterproofed by coating it with gasoline and paraffin.

## THE DEATH OF JUMBO THE ELEPHANT

Standing 11 feet tall, Jumbo was one of the star attractions of the Barnum & Bailey Circus when the celebrated pachyderm was struck and killed by a train at a marshaling yard in St. Thomas, Ontario, Canada, on September 15, 1885. Ever the showman, Barnum told the press at the time that Jumbo had managed to toss a younger elephant to safety right before the train struck, though eyewitness accounts suggest the story isn't true.

Barnum had acquired Jumbo from the London Zoological Gardens for $10,000 in 1882. After Jumbo's death, his skeleton was donated to the American Museum of Natural History in New York City; his heart was sold to Cornell University; and his hide was stuffed and mounted. Barnum continued to exhibit Jumbo's remains until 1889, at which time he donated the stuffed behemoth to Tufts University, where it was displayed until destroyed by a fire in 1975.

## THE DEATH OF KARL WALLENDA

The "Flying Wallendas" were one of the most publicized tightrope acts in modern circus history, dazzling audiences with amazing stunts such as the seven-person chair pyramid. But on March 22, 1978, Karl Wallenda, the family's 73-year-old patriarch, fell to his death during a promotional tightrope walk in San Juan, Puerto Rico. His was not the first family tragedy—Karl's sister-in-law, Rietta Wallenda, fell to her death in 1963, and his son-in-law, Richard Guzman, was killed in 1972 when he accidentally touched a live wire while holding part of the metal rigging.

# 15 TIPS FOR SURVIVING A SHARK ATTACK

**1. CHECK WITH THE LOCALS:** If you don't want to tangle with a shark, don't go where sharks hang out. If you plan to vacation near the ocean, contact local tourism offices and ask for shark stats in the area.

**2. SKIP THE BLING:** Sharks see contrast well, so wearing bright colors like yellow and orange is not a great idea. Also avoid shiny jewelry as sharks may mistake it for fish scales.

**3. KNOW YOUR SHARKS:** Three species of shark are responsible for most human attacks: great white, tiger, and bull sharks. A hammerhead might freak you out, but it probably won't bite you.

**4. BE ADVENTUROUS, BUT NOT RIDICULOUS:** Who knows why you might choose to swim in murky waters, around harbor entrances or steep drop-offs, or among rocky, underwater cliffs, but if you do choose to swim in these dangerous places, don't be surprised if you come face-to-face with a shark.

**5. SWIM SMART:** Always swim with a buddy, and don't swim at dusk or at night. Sharks don't have the best vision, so when it's dark, you look like dinner to them.

**6. CHECK WITH THE TURTLES:** Creatures of the sea know much more about the waters than you ever will. So, if turtles and fish start freaking out, there's probably a reason. If you witness erratic behavior from other animals, there might be a very large, toothy beast approaching. Take a cue from those who have seen it before and take off.

**7. FOR THE LADIES:** If you're menstruating, stick to the sand. Blood attracts sharks. Female or male, if you cut yourself on a reef or a rock while swimming, it's best to get out right away—the smell of blood to a shark is like the smell of fresh doughnuts to humans.

**8. KEEP FIDO ON THE BEACH:** Allowing dogs to swim in the ocean can be dangerous if you're in shark territory. Animals swim erratically, attracting the attention of sharks. Don't let pets stay in the water for long periods of time.

**9. SHOUT IF YOU SEE A SHARK:** If there's a dorsal fin on the horizon, letting people know is a good idea. The more people know what's going on, the better off you are if the situation worsens. Then quickly swim toward shore as if your life depends on it...because it just might.

**10. SHARK APPROACHING: STAY SILENT AND IMMOBILE:** If you aren't able to get to shore and a shark approaches you, try to stay still and be quiet to avoid an attack.

**11. SHARK ZIGZAGGING: FIND SOMETHING SOLID:** The zigzagging shark is looking for angles, so if you can back up against a reef, a piling, or some other kind of outcropping, do so. This reduces the number of angles the shark has to come at you. If you're in open water, get back-to-back with your swimming buddy. You do have a swimming buddy, right?

**12. SHARK CIRCLING: UH-OH:** This is not good. If a shark is circling you, that means it's about to strike. Time to fight back!

**13. SHARK ATTACKING: THE EYES HAVE IT:** It might sound ridiculous, but try to stay calm. If a shark is attacking you, go for the eyes and gills, the most vulnerable parts of the shark. If you can wound the eyes, you've got a chance.

**14. GO FOR THE NOSE (OR NOT...):** Although opinions differ, the general consensus seems to be that if you can get a clear shot, hitting the shark on the nose can be highly effective at ending the attack. Trouble is, when you're being attacked, hitting a specific target becomes challenging at best.

**15. WHAT NOT TO DO:** Don't play dead. This does nothing but make the shark think it has won. The shark will then commence chomping. Clearly, this is not what you want it to do. Also, if you've been attacked, get away as fast as you possibly can. Since sharks smell blood, there are probably more on the way.

# TRUE TALES OF BEING BURIED ALIVE

## DAVID BLAINE

On April 5, 1999, before an estimated crowd of 75,000 on Manhattan's Upper West Side, magician David Blaine undertook his "Buried Alive" stunt, voluntarily going six feet under, albeit with a small air tube. Placed inside a transparent plastic coffin with a mere six inches of headroom and two inches on either side, the illusionist was lowered into his burial pit. Next, a three-ton water-filled tank was lowered on top of his tomb. The magician ate nothing during his stunt and reportedly only sipped two to three tablespoons of water per day—a fasting schedule likely designed to keep bodily wastes to a minimum. After seven days of self-entombment, Blaine popped out, none the worse for wear. Many believed that the magician had somehow left his tomb and returned only when it was time to emerge. However, these naysayers couldn't explain why he'd been visible the entire time and how witnesses saw him move on a number of occasions. Blaine called it a "test of endurance of…the human body and mind…." Even famous debunker and fellow magic man James Randi praised him.

## BARBARA JANE MACKLE

Could there be anything more horrifying than a forced burial? Emory University student Barbara Jane Mackle suffered through such an ordeal and miraculously lived to tell the tale. Abducted from a motel room on December 17, 1968, the 20-year-old daughter of business mogul Robert Mackle was whisked off to a remote location and buried under 18 inches of earth. Her coffinlike box was sparsely equipped with food, water, a pair of vent tubes, and a light. After receiving their $500,000 ransom, the kidnappers informed the FBI of the girl's location. Some 80 hours after Mackle entered her underground prison, she was discovered in a wooded area roughly 20 miles northeast of Atlanta. Her light source had failed just a few hours after her burial, and she was severely dehydrated, but otherwise the young woman was in good condition. Both kidnappers were eventually apprehended.

## SCHOOL BUS KIDNAPPING AND LIVE BURIAL

A notably bizarre burial occurred in 1976 when an entire school bus filled with children was hijacked in Chowchilla, California. The driver and 26 children were removed from the bus, placed into vans, and driven a hundred miles to a quarry in the town of Livermore. There they were forced into a moving van buried several feet below ground. Limited survival supplies and minimal air vents welcomed them into a pitch-black, claustrophobic hell. After 12 long hours, the students feverishly started looking for ways out. Fashioning a crude ladder out of old mattresses, the bus driver and a group of boys climbed to the top of the moving van where they had originally entered. Using a wooden beam, they were able to slowly pry off the heavy, metal lid that separated them from sweet freedom. After 16 hours below ground, they emerged. Despite their harrowing experience, all survived. A ransom note was eventually traced back to Frederick Woods, the quarry owner's son. He and accomplices Richard and James Schoenfeld were convicted and sentenced to life in prison.

## How Does a Gas Pump Nozzle Know When Your Tank Is Full?

When you've maxed out your credit card, of course. Actually, the system is entirely mechanical and completely ignorant of the gas station's financial needs.

The mechanism at work is a little complicated, but the basic idea is fairly straightforward. As gas flows, it generates suction inside the nozzle, thanks to something called the Venturi effect. A fuel nozzle uses this suction to gauge whether there's any air at the end of the nozzle spout.

In the nozzle, the gas passes through a Venturi ring, a narrow passageway with tiny openings that lead to an air chamber. This air chamber is connected to a long tube that leads to a hole near the end of the nozzle spout, just under the larger hole where the gas comes out. Essentially, this tube is a straw for sucking air from the tank. As the fuel flows through the ring, the suction from the Venturi effect reduces air pressure in the chamber. Air rushes from the tank through the tube to equalize the pressure, in the same way soda rushes through a straw to equalize a drop in pressure in your mouth.

As long as there is room in the tank, the system will keep sucking in air and the pressure in the chamber will stay close to normal atmospheric levels. But when the gasoline reaches the tip of the nozzle, no more air can get through the little hole and the pressure in the chamber drops. This increased suction pulls on a diaphragm connected to the nozzle's shut-off valve, which closes to stop the flow of gasoline.

If you try to keep pumping to "top off" the tank, you might actually be pumping money out of your wallet. According to the Environmental Protection Agency, when there's no room in the tank, extra gas can flow up through vapor recovery lines in the pump that are designed to prevent gas vapor from polluting the atmosphere. As a result, you may be paying to pump gas back into the station's tanks.

## CURIOUS CLASSIFIEDS

- **Job Wanted**—Man, honest. Will take anything.
- **Sale**—Stock up and save. Limit one.
- **Used Cars**—Why go elsewhere to be cheated? Come here first!
- **Christmas Tag Sale**—Handmade gifts for the hard-to-find person.
- **Furniture**—Sofas. Only $299! For rest or fore play.
- **Teacher**—Three-year-old teacher needed for pre-school. Experience preferred.
- **For Sale**—Antique desk suitable for lady with thick legs and large drawers.
- **Grand Opening**—The Superstore—unequaled in size, unmatched in variety, unrivaled inconvenience.
- **For Sale**—Mixing bowl set designed to please a cook with round bottom for efficient beating.
- **Helper**—Tired of cleaning yourself? Let me do it.
- **Auto Repair Service**—Free pick-up and delivery. Try us once, you'll never go anywhere again.

- **For Sale**—Amana washer $100. Owned by clean bachelor who seldom washed.
- **Free Puppies**—Half cocker spaniel, half sneaky neighbor's dog.

# Why Isn't the Whole Plane Made of the Same Stuff as the Black Box?

Planes, believe it or not, are pretty lightweight. They're built with light metals, such as aluminum. The newer ones are built with even lighter composite materials and plastics. This allows them to be fairly sturdy without adding too much weight.

If planes were instead made of the same stuff as the black box, they just wouldn't get off the ground. But let's backtrack a bit here. The term black box is actually a little misleading. What the media refer to as a "black box" is actually two boxes: the Flight Data Recorder (FDR), which records altitude, speed, magnetic heading, and so on; and the Cockpit Voice Recorder (CVR), which records the sounds in the cockpit. What's more, these boxes are generally bright orange, making them easier to find after a crash. "Black" box either comes from older models that were black or from the charred and/or damaged state of the boxes after a crash.

Whatever the reason behind the name, black boxes are sturdy little things. They carry a bunch of microchips and memory banks encased in protective stainless steel. The protective casing is about a quarter-inch thick; it makes the boxes really heavy. A plane would need a lot more fuel to keep itself up if it was made out of such heavy material.

Furthermore, it's not necessarily that black boxes are indestructible—they remain intact after a crash partially because they are well placed. They're generally put in the tail of the plane, which often doesn't bear the brunt of a crash.

Even with this extra protection, black boxes sometimes don't survive a plane crash. Still, they typically have been useful—though not so useful that you'd want to build an entire plane with their stainless steel casings.

# THINGS YOU DON'T KNOW ABOUT THE PENNY

- Since they were introduced in 1787, more than 300 billion pennies have been produced. Today, there are about 150 billion pennies in circulation—enough to circle Earth 137 times.

- Since 1909, Abraham Lincoln has been the star of the penny, but it wasn't always that way. There have been 11 different designs, including the popular Indian Head penny, which was introduced in 1859.

- The princess on the Indian Head penny was neither a Native American nor a princess. She was, in fact, the sculptor's daughter, Sarah Longacre.

- On the 200th anniversary of Lincoln's birth, the U.S. Mint introduced pennies that depicted four different representations of Lincoln's life. These replaced the Lincoln Memorial on the penny.

- Examine the faces on a penny, an original Jefferson nickel, a dime, and a quarter. All the presidents except Lincoln are facing left.

- Pennies haven't been made of pure copper since 1864. During World War II, the U.S. Mint helped the war effort by recycling: It melted shell casings to make pennies. To conserve further, it considered creating plastic pennies but settled on zinc-covered steel. After the war, the Mint returned to a zinc-and-copper combination.

- Money is shrinking—and not just in value. When the penny was introduced in 1787, it was about twice the size of today's version. The penny didn't shrink to its current size until 1857.

- You can't use pennies to pay your fare at tollbooths—unless you're in Illinois. Lincoln's home state has a soft spot for pennies.

- A coin toss isn't a game of luck if you use a penny and call heads. The penny is the only coin with the face of the same person on both sides. A magnifying glass will reveal Lincoln sitting inside the Lincoln Memorial.

- Pennies got their reputation as being lucky from the Victorian wedding saying "Something old, something new, something borrowed, something blue, and a silver sixpence in your shoe." In the United States, the penny replaced the sixpence as a guard against want for the newlywed couple.

# WHO KNEW?

## TOO MUCH WEB SURFING

Studies suggest that Internet addiction is becoming a growing concern in the United States. One report found that one out of every eight people is "addicted" to being online. Addiction, in this case, is defined as a behavior-altering, habit-forming, compulsive, physiological need to use the Internet.

## NOT SO MOBILE

The world's largest functioning mobile phone is the Maxi Handy, which measures 6.72 feet tall by 2.72 feet wide by 1.47 feet deep. This phone was installed at the Rotmain Centre in Bayreuth, Germany, on June 7, 2004, as part of the "Einfach Mobil" (simple mobil) informational tour. Constructed of wood, polyester, and metal, the fully functional phone features a color screen and can send and receive text and multimedia messages.

## MINING FOR DIAMONDS

It's finders keepers at the Crater of Diamonds State Park in Murfreesboro, Arkansas—the world's only public diamond-producing site. Visitors can keep any stones they dig up! The visitor center features exhibits and an audio/visual program that explains the area's geology. The center even offers tips on recognizing diamonds in the rough.

## MADE OF STONE

The Washington Monument is the world's tallest freestanding

stone structure not created from just a single block of stone. The monument is composed of more than 36,000 separate blocks. It stands a whopping 555 feet tall and weighs approximately 90,854 tons! The outside is composed almost entirely of white marble, while the inside is granite.

## Why Does It Take Longer to Fly West Than East?

If you've ever flown a long distance, you might have noticed it takes more time to fly from east to west than west to east. Since there's no real traffic in the sky (apart from the occasional flock of birds), the delay seems inexplicable. It should take the same amount of time to go anywhere, regardless of the direction.

But the truth is, the air up there isn't quite as wide open as it seems. At the high altitude required for commercial flights, there's a powerful, persistent horizontal wind known as the jet stream. Due to the differences in temperature and pressure between the equator and Earth's polar regions, the jet stream flows from west to east in the Northern Hemisphere. This jet stream is a lot like a current in a river: If you're moving with the current, you'll go faster; conversely, working against the current slows you down and makes you work harder to get where you're going.

The airlines take advantage of the jet stream, purposely flying within it on eastbound flights to allow planes to reach their destinations sooner, and with less wear and tear. (Some airlines even offer cheaper fares on the eastbound leg of a journey.) But on a westbound flight, a pilot must fly against the jet stream, which obviously means it takes more time. A westerly cross-country flight lasts about a half-hour longer than its easterly counterpart.

# HOW TO BEAT A LIE DETECTOR TEST

The polygraph or "lie detector" test is one of the most misunderstood tests used in law enforcement and industry.

Many experts will tell you that lie detector tests are based on fallible data—regardless of how scientific the equipment appears, there's no sure way a person can tell whether or not someone is lying. Since the test is so imperfect, be suspicious of anyone who makes your fate contingent upon the results of a polygraph test. Still, here are a few suggestions on how to beat one:

**1.** Unless you're applying for a job, refuse to take the polygraph test. There are no laws that can compel anyone to take it.

**2.** Keep your answers short and to the point. Most questions asked of you can be answered with a "yes" or "no." Keep it simple.

**3.** During the polygraph test, you'll be asked three types of questions—irrelevant, relevant, and control questions. Irrelevant questions generally take the form of, "Is the color of this room white?" Relevant questions are the areas that get you into trouble. Control questions are designed to "calibrate" your responses during the test. See the next point.

**4.** Control questions are asked so that the technician can compare the responses to questions against a known entity. The easiest way to beat a lie detector test is to invalidate the control questions. Try these simple techniques when asked a control question:

- Change your breathing rate and depth from the normal 15 to 30 breaths per minute to anything faster or slower.

- Solve a math problem in your head, or count backward from 100 by 7.

- Bite the sides of your tongue until it begins to hurt.

## POPULAR NOTIONS: TRUE OR FALSE?

### Lemmings commit suicide if their population increases too much.

**FALSE:** This legend emerged after it was staged in the 1958 Disney animal documentary *White Wilderness*.

### The *Titanic* was the first ship to use SOS as a distress signal.

**FALSE:** Ships had been using SOS for at least three years before the *Titanic*'s fateful voyage.

**Charlie Chaplin once entered and lost a
Charlie Chaplin look-alike contest.**

**TRUE:** He even failed to make the finals.

**The American flag must be burned if
it touches the ground.**

**FALSE:** Out of respect, it shouldn't touch the ground, but
it doesn't need to be burned if this happens.

**Two of the "Marlboro Men" featured in
cigarette ads died of lung cancer.**

**TRUE:** Wayne McLaren, who became an anti-smoking activist
after getting lung cancer, died in 1992 at the age of 51.
David McLean, a Marlboro Man from the 1960s, died in
1995 at the age of 73.

**American Express issues a special black card
that allows its holder to buy anything.**

**TRUE:** But it's still not known if the story came before
the card.

**Your dog's age in human years is its
actual age multiplied by seven.**

**FALSE:** This formula works as a rough estimate in a dog's
middle years, but not for its entire life.

**There are more suicides around Christmas
than at any other time of the year.**

**FALSE:** A study conducted over more than 35 years revealed no increase during this holiday.

# Does Running Through the Rain Keep You Drier Than Walking?

It makes intuitive sense that running through the rain will keep you drier than walking. You will spend less time in the rain, after all. But there's a pervasive old wives' tale that says it won't do any good. So every time there's a downpour and you need to get to your car, you are faced with this confounding question: Should you run or walk?

The argument against running is that more drops hit your chest and legs when you're moving at a quicker pace through the rain. If you're walking, the argument goes, the drops are mainly hitting your head. So the proponents of walking say that running exposes you to more drops, not fewer.

Several scientists have pondered this possibility. In 1987, an Italian physicist determined that sprinting keeps you drier than walking, but only by about 10 percent, which might not be worth the effort and the risk of slipping. In 1995, a British researcher concluded that the increased front-drenching of running effectively cancels out the reduced rain exposure. These findings didn't seem right to two climatologists at the National Climatic Data Center in Asheville, North Carolina, so they decided to put them to the test. In 1996, the two meteorologists put on identical outfits with plastic bags underneath to keep moisture from seeping out of the clothes and to keep their own sweat from adding to the drenching.

One ran about 330 feet in the rain; the other walked the same distance. They weighed the wet clothes, compared the weights to those when the clothes were dry, and determined that the walking meteorologist got 40 percent wetter than the running meteorologist.

In other words, run to your car. You're justified—no matter how silly you might look.

# THE STORY OF THE STRAIGHTJACKET

Before progressive psychoanalysis and newer medications, doctors didn't know how to treat mentally ill patients, so they often restrained them in a jacketlike garment with overlong sleeves. The ends of the sleeves went far beyond a patient's hands, and they were secured to the patient's back, keeping his or her arms crossed close to the chest, restricting most arm movement. Many institutional straitjackets are made of canvas or duck cloth for material strength, but modern jackets intended as fetish wear or fashion items often use leather or PVC instead.

The establishment of asylums and the use of straitjackets gained momentum in the early 1800s. Doctors listed such things as religious excitement, sunstroke, and reading novels as possible causes for mental illness. They believed that patients had lost all power over their morals and that strict discipline was necessary to help patients regain self-control.

Escape artists have used straitjackets in their acts for years. Harry Houdini first thought of using the straitjacket in the early 1900s while touring an insane asylum in Canada. He amazed disbelievers by getting out of one in front of live audiences. Later, he turned it into a public spectacle by escaping as he hung upside-down, suspended from a towering skyscraper.

## Why Does a Seashell Sound Like the Ocean?

Is that big spiral conch you picked up during last year's trip to Hawaii still whispering sweet nothings in your ear? Well, that isn't the roar of the blue Pacific you hear—it's nothing more than the barrage of ambient noise around you.

Seashells don't really create any sound all by themselves. Inside, they're a labyrinth of hollow areas and hard, curved surfaces that happen to be really good reflectors of racket.

When you hold a seashell up to your ear, that shell is actually capturing and amplifying all the little noises occurring around you. These noises are usually so hushed that you don't even hear them unless you're paying very close attention. However, when they begin bouncing off the cavity of a shell, the echoes resonate more loudly into your ear. And they sound a lot like ocean waves rolling up to shore.

It doesn't matter how far away you are from the sea, or even if you have a seashell. You can recreate the same "ocean sound" effect by simply cupping your hand, or a coffee mug, over your ear. Just be sure that mug is empty—or you'll really hear a splash.

# FAMILIAR NUMBERS AND THE LOGIC BEHIND THEM

## ZIP CODES

ZIP ("Zoning Improvement Plan") codes were introduced in 1963 as a way to help ease the massive burden on the post office. According to the USPS, this is what your five-digit ZIP code means:

- The first digit represents the geographic area of the country (the higher the number, the farther west).

- The next two digits represent the "sectional facility"—one of several hundred major distribution centers maintained by the post office.

- The last two digits represent the individual post office or zoning area.

## SOCIAL SECURITY NUMBERS

The social security number may seem like a random string of nine digits, but there is actually logic behind it.

- The first three digits are called the "area number" and were originally supposed to represent the state in which the card was issued, though now they are based on the ZIP code of the applicant.

- The two digits that follow the area number are known as the "group number." These numbers are issued based on a convoluted odd/even numbering sequence. The logic of the group number defies explanation.

- The last four digits are known as a "serial number." These numbers are issued consecutively from 0000 to 9999 within each group.

# 666

Any fan of horror movies can tell you that there's nothing good about the number 666. But they might be less certain about the reason why the number is associated with the Devil. The number 666—also known as the Number of the Beast—gets its evil connotation from the Book of Revelation in the New Testament, specifically in chapter 13, verse 18: "Wisdom is needed here; one who understands can calculate the number of the beast, for it is a number that stands for a person. His number is six hundred and sixty-six." Thus, the number of both the Devil and the Antichrist is revealed to be 666.

Many people have noted that this is unusually specific for a book that otherwise deals with what are presumably symbols, such as dragons coming out of the earth and fire shooting from the sky. As with the interpretation of the Book of Revelation in general, there has been a lot of debate about the precise meaning of this number.

On one side, there is the lunatic fringe, which ascribes the sign of the beast to whichever public figure has raised its ire. In the 1980s, for example, some malcontents pointed out that President Reagan's full name—Ronald Wilson Reagan—is composed of three six-letter groupings.

A more sane theory attributes the number 666 to the Roman emperor Nero. Nero blamed the Christians for the infamous burning of Rome in the first century A.D., and consequently started a brutal campaign of persecution against the fledgling religion. It is believed that the author of the Book of Revelation, John the Apostle, was attempting to send a coded message to his fellow Christians to give them hope that Nero's tyranny would soon come to an end.

To ensure that only other Christians would understand his message, John used Hebrew numerology. John chose Hebrew because it is the language of Judaism, the religion that Christianity grew out of after the arrival of Christ. In Hebrew, each letter corresponds with a number. The letters/numbers from Nero's full name in Hebrew, Neron Qeisar, add up to—you guessed it—666.